THE
COUNTRY WOMEN'S
ASSOCIATION
COOK 2
BOOK 2

THE
COUNTRY WOMEN'S
ASSOCIATION

COOK
BOOK 2

More treasured recipes

MURDOCH BOOKS

Published in 2011 by Murdoch Books Pty Limited

Murdoch Books Australia
Pier 8/9
23 Hickson Road
Millers Point NSW 2000
Phone: +61 (0) 2 8220 2000
Fax: +61 (0) 2 8220 2558
www.murdochbooks.com.au

Murdoch Books UK Limited
Erico House, 6th Floor
93–99 Upper Richmond Road
Putney, London SW15 2TG
Phone: +44 (0) 20 8785 5995
Fax: +44 (0) 20 8785 5985
www.murdochbooks.co.uk

Food Publisher: Kylie Walker
Project Manager and Editor: Janine Flew
Food Editor: Grace Campbell
Food Consultant: Pauline Hunt
Concept and Design: Katy Wall
Production: Renée Melbourne

National Library of Australia Cataloguing-in-Publication entry
Title: The Country Womens Association cookbook 2
ISBN: 9781741969290 (hbk.)
Notes: Includes index
Subjects: Cooking
Other Authors/Contributors:
Country Women's Association of New South Wales
Dewey Number: 641.5

The Country Women's Association of NSW and Murdoch Books would like to thank
the following CWA members for kindly contributing new recipes to this book:
Ann Adams, Gai Bailey, Marj Byrnes, Marie Cantrill, Jennifer Connolly, Patricia
Godfrey, Alison Hordern, Janet Klepatzki, Anita Knight, Alison Lehmann, Helen
Morison, Robyn Peters, Margaret Roberts, Barbara Scanes, Eileen Shepherd,
Stephanie Tuckwell, Patricia Williams and Morna Wilson.

Printed by 1010 Printing International Limited.
PRINTED IN CHINA. Reprinted 2011.

Contents

Introduction 7

Snacks and starters 8

Soups and sandwiches 24

Quiches, pies and savoury tarts 42

Main dishes 54

Salads and side vegetables 90

Desserts 110

Cakes and muffins 130

Biscuits and slices 166

Breads 200

Jams and confectionery 212

Sauces and preserves 228

Exhibition tips 242

Catering hints 244

Measuring up 245

Index 246

Top to bottom; Delegates at State conference; Broken Hill 1952; Menindee 1928, Mudgee Rest Rooms

Introduction

The Country Women's Association of New South Wales, including ACT, is part of the largest female lobby group in Australia (the CWA of Australia), and is well represented, with approximately 11,000 members belonging to 430 branches.

Throughout New South Wales and the ACT, branches meet monthly to take on any number of initiatives – be it fundraising for medical research, lobbying for better services for families or helping out in times of emergency, as well as handicraft and cookery projects.

Starting from humble beginnings in 1922, the CWA of New South Wales is still looking and listening for ways to improve the opportunities for women and their families in local communities.

The CWA not only provides an opportunity for women to share experiences and skills in cooking and handicrafts but also brings people together in friendship to solve problems that affect women and their families.

In its 88-year history, some very significant changes have been made to government policies, roads, education, health and family living standards that can be attributed to the work of CWA members. In an excerpt from *Serving the Country*, a CWA of New South Wales history book, author Helen Townsend writes, 'sixty years ago, if a community needed a hospital, the CWA would roll up its sleeves and get one built. Now if a community needs a hospital, organisations such as the CWA must roll up their sleeves and go and ask the Government to build one.'

The CWA of New South Wales is evolving to work in new environments, but still under the same banner of improving conditions and life for women, children and families.

For more information, see our website www.cwaofnsw.org.au or telephone 02 9358 2923.

Tamworth, 1924

Snacks
and
starters

Curry rice puffs

2½ cups cooked white rice
180 g tin red or pink salmon
2 eggs
½ cup self-raising flour
2 tablespoons finely chopped parsley
1 clove garlic, crushed (optional)
2 tablespoons lemon juice
Dry breadcrumbs, for coating
Vegetable oil, for frying

Combine all ingredients except breadcrumbs and oil. Mix well. If too stiff, thin with a little milk. Cover and chill thoroughly. Shape mixture into walnut-sized balls, then coat in breadcrumbs. Shallow-fry or deep-fry in hot oil until crisp and golden. Drain and serve. Serve alone, or with yoghurt and mint or a sweet-and-sour sauce.

Marinated chicken wings

1.5 kg chicken wings
¼ cup soy sauce
1 clove garlic or 1 teaspoon crushed garlic
2 tablespoons dry sherry
1 teaspoon grated ginger
2 teaspoons brown sugar
1 tablespoon honey
Salt and pepper

Separate chicken wings at the joints into three pieces and discard the tips. Mix remaining ingredients together and combine with chicken in a bowl. Cover and refrigerate overnight, stirring once or twice. Pour chicken and marinade into a baking dish. Bake in a moderate oven for 35–40 minutes. Serve hot or cold as an appetiser.

Spanish tortilla

½ cup olive oil
2 large all-purpose potatoes, cut into 5 mm slices
2 large onions, sliced
3 eggs
Salt and pepper

Heat the oil in a 20 cm diameter deep non-stick frying pan with a lid. Place alternate layers of potato and onion in the pan, cover and cook for 8 minutes over low heat. Using tongs, turn the layers in sections (it doesn't matter if they break up). Cover and cook for a further 8 minutes, without allowing the potato to colour.

Put a strainer over a bowl and drain the potato mixture, reserving 1 tablespoon of the oil.

Put the eggs and a little salt and pepper in a bowl and whisk to combine. Add the potato mixture, pressing down with the back of a spoon to completely cover with the egg.

Heat the reserved oil in the same frying pan over high heat. Pour in the egg mixture, pressing down to even it out. Reduce the heat to low, cover with a lid and cook for 12 minutes, or until set. Gently shake the pan to ensure the tortilla is not sticking. Leave to cook for 5 minutes, then invert onto a plate. Cut into wedges. Serve at room temperature.

Salmon pâté

½ cup hot water
1 tablespoon gelatine
220 g tin red salmon
2 spring onions, roughly chopped
¼ cup mayonnaise
2 teaspoons lemon juice
Salt and pepper
½ cup cream
Lettuce leaves, to serve

MELBA TOASTS
1 square loaf unsliced bread

Place hot water and gelatine in a blender and blend on high for 1 minute.
Add undrained salmon, spring onions, mayonnaise, lemon juice and salt
and pepper to taste. Blend for another minute. Add cream and blend for
30 seconds. Pour salmon mixture into a lightly oiled mould and refrigerate
until set. To serve, turn out onto lettuce leaves and present with melba
toast triangles.

To make melba toasts, remove all crusts from loaf of bread. Cut loaf in half
widthways (this makes it is easier to cut individual slices). Cut each piece
diagonally in half, giving four thick triangle-shaped pieces of bread. Place
flat side down on board and cut into wafer-thin slices using an electric
knife or serrated knife. Place triangles on ungreased baking trays. Bake at
180°C for 15–20 minutes, turning frequently, until crisp and golden. Melba
toast will keep well for about two weeks if stored in an airtight container.

Savoury cakes

1 egg
1 cup milk
½ cup self-raising flour
1 cup grated cheese
100 g chopped bacon
1 tablespoon chopped parsley

Beat egg and add to milk. In another bowl, sift flour, then add the cheese, bacon and parsley. Pour in milk and egg and mix well. Place dessertspoonfuls into greased mini muffin tins. Bake in a moderate oven for 15 minutes. Makes 24.

Savoury sticks

2 sheets frozen puff pastry, thawed
1 egg, beaten
Sundried tomato paste or olive paste
Grated parmesan cheese
Cayenne pepper (optional)
Poppy or sesame seeds
Grated tasty cheese, extra

Cut each sheet of pastry in half and brush with egg. Spread one side of the pastry with a filling based on sun-dried tomato paste or olive paste and parmesan cheese. Sprinkle with cayenne pepper. Press the two sides of the pastry together firmly with a rolling pin. Cut into strips about 1 cm wide. Twist strips into loose corkscrews and place on a baking tray. Brush with more egg. Sprinkle with poppy or sesame seeds. Bake in a hot oven until golden brown (about 10 minutes), adding extra cheese when almost ready.

Seafood pâté

250 g smoked salmon or hot smoked trout or mackerel
250 g cream cheese
1 tablespoon lemon juice
1 tablespoon grated onion
1 tablespoon tomato sauce or 3 tablespoons mayonnaise
¼ teaspoon Worcestershire sauce

Finely chop fish or mince in a blender. If using a blender, add remaining ingredients and blend again. Alternatively, place remaining ingredients in a bowl and thoroughly mix, then mix in fish. Place in a 500 ml container or shape as desired. Chill. Serve with crackers or as a spread.

Tuna toasties

1 loaf sliced bread
Butter, softened, for spreading
185 g tin tuna in brine, drained
1 small onion, chopped
1 teaspoon curry powder
1 cup thick mayonnaise
Salt and pepper, to taste
Paprika

Remove crusts from bread and spread butter on both sides of bread. Combine all other ingredients except paprika and mix well. Place a spoonful of the mixture diagonally across bread, then roll one corner to the opposite corner and secure with toothpicks. Sprinkle with paprika, then cook at 200°C for 15–20 minutes, until toasted.

Chusuolettes

3 bacon rashers
3 eggs
60 g self-raising flour
125 g grated cheese
1 medium onion, finely chopped
Salt and pepper, to taste
Oil, for frying

Remove fat from the bacon rashers and finely chop the bacon. In a medium-sized bowl combine all ingredients except oil. Mix well. Heat oil in a pan and drop in tablespoonfuls of the mixture. Fry until crisp and golden brown. Drain well and serve hot. Serve with tomato and lettuce salad. Makes 10 patties.

Herb mustard rolls

125 g butter, softened
1 tablespoon seeded mustard
2 tablespoons fresh parsley, chopped
2 tablespoons fresh chives, chopped
1 teaspoon grated lemon zest
6 round white dinner rolls

Combine butter, mustard, parsley, chives and zest in a medium bowl and mix well. Cut rolls in half crossways and spread butter mixture evenly onto each half. Place rolls, buttered side up, onto an oven tray, then bake in a moderate oven for 10 minutes, or until lightly browned. Rolls can be prepared a day ahead. Keep covered in the refrigerator, or freeze for up to 1 month. Unsuitable to microwave.

Corn fritters

60 g butter
½ cup plain flour
2 eggs, lightly beaten
¼ cup tinned creamed corn
Salt and pepper
1 tablespoon grated parmesan cheese
Oil, for deep-frying

Combine butter with ½ cup water in a small pan and stir until butter has melted. Bring to boil, then remove from the heat. Stir in the flour. Return pan to heat and stir until mixture leaves the sides of the pan. Transfer to a mixing bowl. Cool slightly, then gradually add the beaten eggs. Beat with electric mixers until mixture is smooth, thick and shiny. Beat in the creamed corn, salt, pepper and cheese. Making only two or three fritters at a time, drop level tablespoons of the mixture into moderately hot oil. Cook until golden and doubled in size. Remove and drain on paper towel.

Bruschetta

5 finely diced roma tomatoes
1 medium Spanish onion, finely diced
Pinch sugar
8 fresh basil leaves, torn
50 ml balsamic vinegar
100 ml olive oil
1 French bread breadstick, to serve
20 g Danish feta cheese, crumbled or thinly sliced, to garnish
Salt and pepper, to taste

Combine tomato, onion, sugar and basil. Marinate in vinegar and oil for 10–20 minutes. Slice the French breadstick into pieces diagonally and warm in the oven. Top with the tomato mixture, garnish with feta and season to taste.

This makes a nice starter – use very fresh basil and roma tomatoes, for a good flavour.

Savoury pinwheels

2 sheets frozen puff pastry
500 g pork mince
½ teaspoon curry powder
2 tablespoons mango chutney
1 onion, finely chopped

Thaw pastry. Place all remaining ingredients in a bowl and mix well, then season. Spread onto pastry sheets and roll as for a Swiss roll. Cut into 1 cm wide pieces, place on greased trays and bake at 200°C for 20–25 minutes, turning once. Serve hot or cold.

Chilli nuts

2–3 tablespoons oil
6 large pappadams, broken into pieces
2 cups Rice Bubbles
2 cups sultanas
250 g salted cashews
250 g salted peanuts
Pinch chilli powder, or to taste

Heat oil in pan. Add pappadam pieces, stirring until cooked and puffed. Add Rice Bubbles and cook for 1 minute. Stir in sultanas, cashews and peanuts. Cook for 2 minutes, stirring constantly. Remove from heat, then stir in chilli powder. Cool. Store in an airtight container. Makes 10 cups.

Sausage rolls

3 sheets frozen puff pastry, thawed
2 eggs, lightly beaten
750 g sausage mince
1 onion, finely chopped
1 garlic clove, crushed
1 cup fresh breadcrumbs
3 tablespoons chopped flat-leaf (Italian) parsley
3 tablespoons chopped thyme
½ teaspoon ground sage
½ teaspoon freshly grated nutmeg
½ teaspoon ground cloves
½ teaspoon pepper

Preheat the oven to 200°C. Lightly grease two baking trays.

Cut the pastry sheets in half and lightly brush the edges with some of the beaten egg.

Mix half the remaining egg with the remaining ingredients in a large bowl, then divide into six even portions. Pipe or spoon filling down the centre of each piece of pastry, then brush edges with some of the egg. Fold the pastry over the filling, overlapping the edges and placing the join underneath. Brush the rolls with more egg, then cut each into six short pieces.

Cut two small slashes on top of each roll, place on the baking trays and bake for 15 minutes. Reduce the heat to 180°C and bake for another 15 minutes, or until puffed and golden.

Barbecue honey chicken wings

12 chicken wings
4 tablespoons soy sauce
3 tablespoons sherry
3 tablespoons oil
1 garlic clove, crushed
3 tablespoons honey

Rinse the chicken wings, then pat dry thoroughly with paper towels. Tuck the wing tips into the underside.

Put the chicken wings in a shallow non-metallic dish. In a bowl, whisk together the soy sauce, sherry, oil and garlic, then pour all over the chicken wings, lightly tossing. Cover with plastic wrap, then marinate in the refrigerator for 2 hours, turning occasionally.

Warm the honey until it is of brushing consistency.

Lightly grease a barbecue or chargrill pan and heat it up. Lift the chicken out of the marinade and add it to the hot pan. Cook the chicken wings until tender and cooked through, turning occasionally — this should take about 12 minutes. Now brush the wings with the warmed honey and cook for a further 2 minutes.

Cheese and bacon straws

1 teaspoon oil
4 bacon rashers, finely chopped
2 sheets ready-rolled puff pastry, thawed
1 egg, lightly beaten
1 cup grated tasty cheese
2 spring onions, chopped
1 tablespoon chopped parsley
1 teaspoon paprika

Heat oil in a pan. Add bacon and cook until crisp; leave to drain on absorbent paper.

Brush pastry sheets with a little egg, then sprinkle a quarter of the cheese over half of each sheet, leaving a 1 cm border. Sprinkle with combined bacon, spring onions, parsley, paprika and remaining cheese. Fold sheets in half to enclose filling. Press together lightly, then brush surface with a little more egg. Cut crossways into 1 cm strips. Twist strips, then place about 3 cm apart onto greased trays.

Bake at 200°C for about 12 minutes or until lightly browned; allow to cool on wire racks. Makes about 40.

Guacamole

3 ripe avocados
1 tablespoon lime or lemon juice (see Hint)
1 tomato
1–2 red chillies, finely chopped
1 small red onion, finely chopped
1 tablespoon finely chopped coriander (cilantro) leaves
2 tablespoons sour cream
1–2 drops Tabasco sauce
Pepper
Corn chips, to serve

Roughly chop the avocado flesh and place in a bowl. Mash lightly with a fork and sprinkle with juice to prevent the avocado from discolouring.

Cut the tomato in half horizontally and use a teaspoon to scoop out the seeds. Finely dice the flesh and add to the avocado.

Stir in the chilli, onion, coriander, sour cream and Tabasco sauce. Season with pepper.

Serve immediately or cover the surface with plastic wrap and refrigerate for 1–2 hours. If refrigerated, allow to come to room temperature before serving. Serve with corn chips.

HINT: You will need 1–2 limes to produce 1 tablespoon of juice, depending on the lime. A heavier lime will probably be juicier. To get more juice from a citrus fruit, prick it all over with a fork and then heat on high (100%) in the microwave for 1 minute. Don't forget to prick it or the fruit may burst.

Savoury potato empanadas

¼ cup olive oil
1 small onion, finely diced
2 spring onions (scallions), thinly sliced
1 garlic clove, crushed
100 g beef mince
1 teaspoon ground cumin
1 teaspoon dried oregano
½ teaspoon salt
½ teaspoon pepper
125 g all-purpose potatoes, diced
4 sheets frozen puff pastry, thawed
50 g black olives, pitted and quartered
1 hard-boiled egg, finely chopped
1 egg, separated
Pinch paprika
Pinch sugar

In a frying pan, heat 1 tablespoon oil. Add onion and spring onion, stir for 5 minutes; add garlic and stir for 3 minutes. Remove from pan and set aside. Heat remaining oil, add beef and stir over medium heat until browned, breaking up any lumps with a fork. Stir in the onion mixture.

Add cumin, oregano, salt and pepper. Stir for 2 minutes. Transfer to a bowl and cool. Wipe out the pan with paper towel. Heat another tablespoon of oil in the pan, add potato and stir over high heat for 1 minute. Reduce heat to low and stir for 5 minutes, or until tender. Cool slightly and then gently mix into the beef mixture.

Preheat oven to 200°C. Lightly grease two baking trays. Cut 8 cm rounds from pastry. Spoon heaped teaspoons of the beef mixture onto one side of each pastry round, leaving a border. Put a few olive quarters and some chopped egg on top of the beef mixture. Brush border with egg white. Fold pastry over to make a half moon shape, pressing firmly to seal. Flatten the edges with a floured fork, then transfer to baking trays. Combine egg yolk, paprika and sugar and brush over the empanadas. Bake for 15 minutes, or until golden brown and puffed.

Evans Head Seaside Cottage

Soups
and
sandwiches

Chicken stock

Chicken bones or trimmings
Lemon juice
Bay leaf
Black pepper

Combine all ingredients with 2 litres water and bring to the boil. Simmer for 1 hour and strain. Remove bay leaf. Refrigerate or freeze.

Spring chicken soup

1 litre vegetable stock
2 tablespoons baby peas
40 g instant noodles
1 carrot, grated
1 spring onion, finely sliced
1 chicken breast, finely sliced
1 small teaspoon chicken stock powder
Pinch onion powder
Pinch celery powder
Pinch salt

Bring stock to the boil, then add peas and noodles. Re-boil stock, then add carrot and onion. Simmer for 3–5 minutes. Add chicken, chicken stock powder, onion powder, celery powder and salt, and heat through. Serve in heated bowls with freshly baked scones.

Ginger carrot soup

30 g butter or margarine
4 cups sliced carrots
1 large onion, chopped
2 teaspoons grated orange peel
1 teaspoon grated fresh ginger or ¼ teaspoon ground ginger
3 cups chicken stock
½ cup milk
1 or 2 tablespoons orange juice
Salt and pepper
Thin orange or lemon slices, or parsley, to garnish

Melt butter in a saucepan over a low heat. Add carrots, onion, orange peel and ginger and cook gently for 5 minutes, stirring occasionally. Add stock and heat mixture until it boils. Reduce heat immediately, cover and simmer for 10 minutes. Purée mixture in batches in a blender until smooth. Return to saucepan, stir in milk, then orange juice. Heat gently to serving temperature. Season to taste, garnish and serve.

Goulash soup

1 heaped teaspoon lard or oil
400 g beef shin or rump, cut into 2 cm cubes
2 chopped onions
1 heaped teaspoon hot paprika
1 level teaspoon salt
400 g potatoes, diced

Melt lard or heat oil in a saucepan and gently sauté beef and onion. When onion is transparent, add the paprika, stir, then pour in 2 litres water. Bring to the boil; add salt. Lower heat, cover the pan and simmer for 1½ hours or until meat is almost tender. Add potatoes and cook until both meat and potatoes are tender.

Hungarian goulash soup

1 tablespoon lard or oil
2 onions, chopped
½ teaspoon ground caraway seeds (optional)
400 g beef shin or rump, diced
1 carrot, sliced
2 green or red capsicums, sliced
1 tomato, peeled and chopped
1 parsley root or parsnip
1 clove garlic, crushed
1 teaspoon medium hot or hot paprika
500 g potatoes, diced
Salt

CSIPETKE (PINCHED DOUGH)
1 egg
5 heaped tablespoons plain flour

Melt the lard or heat the oil in a pan and fry onion gently until golden. Sprinkle with caraway seeds. Add meat, carrot, capsicums, tomato, parsley root, garlic and paprika. Cover pan and leave to simmer. As juices evaporate, gradually add about 2 litres of water to achieve desired consistency. After about 2 hours, add potatoes and bring to the boil. Add salt to taste. Make the csipetke (see below) and add to soup.

To make csipetke, beat egg and mix with sifted flour to make a stiff dough. Roll or pull small pieces of dough (about the size of a hazelnut) from the mixture and drop into boiling soup about 5 minutes before soup is ready. When the csipetke rise to the surface, the goulash is ready to serve.

Nameko (Japanese golden mushroom soy soup)

100 g soy paste
1 teaspoon mirin wine
1½ cups dashi
100 g nameko (golden mushrooms)
250 g tofu, diced
1 shallot stalk, chopped

Combine soy paste, mirin and dashi in a saucepan and heat gently to make soy soup. Divide the nameko and the diced tofu into soup bowls. Using a ladle, pour hot soy soup over the nameko and tofu. Sprinkle chopped shallots over each bowl as a garnish. This soup can also be served after the main meal, as it cleanses the palate. Serves 5.

Pea and ham soup

2 cups dried split peas (see Note)
1 kg ham shanks or bones
2 onions, minced or finely chopped
2 bay leaves
Salt and pepper, to taste
2 cups milk
2 tablespoons flour, sifted

Wash peas and soak in 1.5 litres water overnight. Place ham, peas, water in which peas were soaked, onions, bay leaves, and salt and pepper in a pressure cooker. Cover and pressure cook for 20 minutes. Allow cooker to cool slowly. Add milk to flour and beat until smooth before adding to soup. Cook uncovered for 2–3 minutes until thickened.

NOTE: This soup can be made satisfactorily without soaking peas, if 15 minutes more cooking time in the pressure cooker is allowed.

Pumpkin soup

2 medium onions, diced
4 bacon rashers, diced
1 clove garlic, crushed
3 cups diced pumpkin
1 tablespoon tomato paste
3 cups chicken stock
1 bay leaf
Salt and pepper, to taste
Pinch cayenne pepper
½ cup evaporated milk

Fry onions and bacon in oil. Add garlic, pumpkin, tomato paste and stock. Bring to the boil, adding bay leaf, salt, pepper and cayenne. Cover and simmer for 25 minutes. Remove from heat and allow to cool. Remove bay leaf and put mixture through blender. Return to saucepan, add evaporated milk and heat slowly.

Pumpkin and lentil soup

500 g peeled and diced pumpkin
¾ cup dried red lentils
2 teaspoons chicken stock powder
1 teaspoon ground cumin
4 lean bacon rashers, finely chopped
Parsley, to garnish

Place all ingredients except the bacon and parsley in a large saucepan along with 1.5 litres of water. Bring to the boil, then simmer for 45 minutes, skimming when necessary. Allow to stand and cool. Purée and add more water or stock for the desired consistency. Cook bacon until crisp. Sprinkle bacon and parsley over soup and serve. Serves 4–6.

Pumpkin and orange soup

30 g butter
1 medium onion, chopped
1–2 tablespoons freshly grated ginger
1.5 kg pumpkin, unpeeled
Grated zest and juice of 1 large orange
1.5 litres chicken stock
Salt and pepper, to taste
Cream (optional)
Nutmeg
Pumpkin seeds, toasted (see Note)

Melt butter in a large pan and sauté the onion and ginger until soft. Peel pumpkin and cut into chunks, reserving the seeds. Place pumpkin in the pan with orange zest, juice and chicken stock. Bring to the boil, cover and simmer gently until pumpkin is cooked (about 20 minutes). Purée in batches in a blender or food processor and return to pan. Season to taste. Return to the boil. Divide among bowls, garnish with a swirl of cream. Sprinkle with fresh nutmeg and toasted pumpkin seeds and serve.

Note: To toast pumpkin seeds, rinse well, removing excess pulp. Place on a baking sheet and toast in a moderate oven for 20 minutes. Add a little salt. These also make a tasty snack on their own. Serves 6.

Zucchini soup

50 g butter or margarine
1 kg zucchini, coarsely chopped
2 or 3 sticks celery, diced
2 medium brown onions, chopped finely
2 medium potatoes, coarsely chopped
3 carrots, finely chopped
1 teaspoon salt, or to taste
Pepper
1 small garlic clove, crushed (optional)
4 cups chicken stock
1 teaspoon fresh or dried tarragon leaves
Cream, to serve
Chopped parsley, to serve

Melt butter or margarine in a large saucepan. Add vegetables and toss until well coated. Cook for 5 minutes on low heat with the lid on, but do not allow to brown. Add salt, plenty of pepper and the crushed garlic if using. Pour in the chicken stock and the dried tarragon, if using. Simmer for approximately 15 minutes, or until vegetables are softened.

Put all ingredients through a blender, return to saucepan and add the fresh tarragon, if using. Heat soup and serve with a small dollop of cream in centre and sprinkled with chopped parsley.

This recipe is ideal for using up the excess from a crop of home-grown zucchini.

Tomato, lentil and coriander soup

½ tablespoon oil
1 medium onion, chopped
1 or 2 garlic cloves, crushed (or use bottled garlic)
½ teaspoon ground cumin
¼ teaspoon garam masala
¼ teaspoon chilli flakes
¼ cup tomato paste
800 g tin crushed tomatoes
3 cups vegetable stock
½ cup red lentils (or more if liked)
1 teaspoon sugar
¼ cup fresh coriander leaves (or use tube coriander)

CORIANDER YOGHURT
1 cup plain yoghurt
2 tablespoons chopped parsley
2 tablespoons chopped coriander leaves
1 teaspoon ground coriander

For the soup, heat the oil in a large saucepan. Add the onion, garlic and spices. Cook over medium heat, stirring, until the onion is soft.

Add tomato paste, tomatoes, stock, lentils, sugar and coriander. Simmer, uncovered, for about 20 minutes or until lentils are tender. Serve with coriander yoghurt.

For the coriander yoghurt, combine all ingredients in small bowl and mix well.

Tofu and shiitake mushroom soup

200 g organic udon noodles
1 tablespoon vegetable oil
1 garlic clove, minced
2 teaspoons minced ginger
2 teaspoons miso paste
400 g shiitake mushrooms (fresh or dried)
1 bunch choy sum, roughly chopped
2 tablespoons oyster sauce
2 tablespoons soy sauce
200 g firm tofu
1 litre chicken stock

Prepare udon noodles according to the directions. Drain and set aside.
In a large pot over medium heat add oil, garlic, ginger and miso paste
and cook for about 1 minute. Add mushrooms, choy sum, oyster and soy
sauces and cook for further 2–3 minutes or until choy sum has softened.
Add tofu and stock and simmer for 10 minutes. Serve up an equal quantity
of noodles in four bowls and ladle soup over the top.

Fast mushroom soup

60 g butter
2 onions, chopped
500 g button mushrooms, chopped
¼ cup plain flour
2 cups milk
1½ cups vegetable stock
Sour cream, to serve
Chopped flat-leaf (Italian) parsley, to serve

Heat the butter in a saucepan and fry the onions for 5 minutes, or until they are lightly golden. Add the mushrooms and cook for a further 5 minutes, stirring frequently. Add the flour and stir for 1 minute. Stir in the milk and vegetable stock. Reduce the heat and simmer, uncovered, for 10–15 minutes, or until the soup has thickened and the mushrooms are tender. Serve in bowls, topped with a dollop of sour cream and parsley.

Swiss brown mushrooms can replace the button mushrooms — or, for a stronger flavour, use field mushrooms.

Corn chowder

90 g butter
2 large onions, finely chopped
1 garlic clove, crushed
2 teaspoons cumin seeds
1 litre vegetable stock
2 potatoes, chopped
250 g tin creamed corn
400 g corn kernels
3 tablespoons chopped flat-leaf (Italian) parsley
1 cup grated cheddar cheese
Salt and pepper
2 tablespoons snipped chives, to garnish

Heat the butter in large heavy-based saucepan. Add the onions and cook over medium–high heat for 5 minutes, or until golden. Add the garlic and cumin seeds, cook for 1 minute, stirring constantly. Add the vegetable stock and bring to the boil. Add the potatoes and reduce the heat. Simmer, uncovered, for 10 minutes.

Add the creamed corn, corn kernels and parsley. Bring to the boil, then reduce the heat and simmer for 10 minutes. Stir through the cheese and season to taste. Heat gently until the cheese melts. Serve immediately, sprinkled with the chives.

Leek and potato soup

Cooking oil spray
2 leeks, white part only, sliced
3 cloves garlic, crushed
1 teaspoon ground cumin
1 kg potatoes, chopped
1.25 litres vegetable stock
½ cup skim milk
Salt and pepper

Lightly spray a non-stick frying pan with oil. Add the leek, garlic and 1 tablespoon water to prevent sticking, then cook over low heat, stirring frequently, for 25 minutes, or until the leek turns golden. Add the cumin and cook for 2 minutes.

Put the potato in a large pan with the leek mixture and stock, bring to the boil, reduce the heat and simmer for 10–15 minutes, or until tender. Purée in a processor or blender until smooth. Return to the pan.

Stir in the milk, season and heat through before serving.

Leek and potato soup can also be served cold as a summer starter.

Crunchy tuna rolls

425 g tin tuna
1 onion, grated
2 tablespoons mayonnaise
Pepper, to taste
12 slices bread, crusts removed
Butter for spreading
½ cup cream
½ cup grated cheese

Drain tuna, add onion, mayonnaise and pepper and mix well. Spread each slice of bread with butter, then tuna mixture. Roll up and secure with a toothpick. Pack well into a shallow greased dish, brush with cream and sprinkle the cheese over the top. Bake in a hot oven for 30 minutes or until golden brown.

Turkey and brie triangles

8 slices white bread
100 g cranberry sauce
120 g sliced turkey breast
120 g brie, sliced
4 butter lettuce leaves

Trim the crusts from the bread. Spread four slices with cranberry sauce. Add the turkey breast, brie and lettuce leaves and top with the other four bread slices. Cut each sandwich into four triangles to serve.

Chicken, rocket and walnut sandwiches

2 tablespoons oil
250 g chicken breast
500 g chicken thigh
250 g whole-egg mayonnaise
100 g celery, finely chopped
90 g chopped walnuts
Salt and pepper
20 slices bread
1 large handful rocket (arugula)

Heat the oil in a frying pan over medium heat and cook the chicken breast and thigh until lightly browned. Allow to cool, then chop finely.

Combine chicken with mayonnaise, celery and walnuts. Season to taste.

Make sandwiches using the chicken mixture and add the rocket to each. Remove the crusts and cut each sandwich into three fingers. Makes 30.

Smoked salmon and caper bruschetta

1 baguette or crusty Italian loaf
Olive oil, for brushing
250 g cream cheese
2 tablespoons lemon juice
15 g snipped chives
100 g smoked salmon, sliced
2 tablespoons baby capers, rinsed
2 dill sprigs, to garnish

Cut the bread into 1 cm slices, brush with olive oil and grill until golden on both sides.

Mix the cream cheese with the lemon juice and chives. Spread over the toast and top with small slices of smoked salmon and a few baby capers. Garnish with sprigs of dill before serving. Makes about 24.

Salted capers have a better flavour
and texture than those preserved in brine.
Rinse them before using.

International Day Fete, 1939, Cumberland younger set

Quiches,
pies and
savoury tarts

Helen's quick spinach quiche

2 tablespoons butter
1 small bunch spinach, chopped
1 onion, chopped
2 rashers bacon
1 cup grated tasty cheese
2 eggs
2 tablespoons plain flour, sifted
2 cups milk

Melt butter in a frying pan and fry spinach and onion. Grill bacon. Sprinkle cheese on the bottom of a greased medium quiche dish. Top with spinach, onion and chopped bacon. Beat eggs with flour and milk. Pour over spinach mixture and bake in a moderate oven for 40 minutes.

Savoury pie

4 eggs
2 cups milk (or 1 cup cream and 1 cup milk)
½ cup self-raising flour, sifted
1 onion, finely chopped
¼ cup chopped parsley
200 g tin tuna or salmon, drained
½ cup grated tasty cheese
Pepper to taste

In a large bowl beat together eggs, milk and flour. Stir in remaining ingredients. Pour into a well-greased 30 cm pie dish and bake in moderate oven for 35–40 minutes or until top is browned. Serve hot or cold.

Swiss quiche

PASTRY
1⅓ cups plain flour
Pinch salt
Pinch paprika
250 g butter
125 g grated cheese
1 egg yolk, slightly beaten

FILLING
340 g can asparagus cuts, drained, or 250 g fresh asparagus,
  lightly cooked and cut into lengths
125 g chopped ham (see Variation)
4 eggs
1 tablespoon plain flour
¼ teaspoon salt
Pinch paprika
½ cup milk
1 cup sour cream
125 g grated cheese (optional)

To make pastry, sift flour, salt and paprika, rub in butter, add grated cheese (100 g gruyère and 25 g parmesan makes a good blend) and mix in egg yolk to make a dry dough. Roll out. Use to line a greased 20 cm quiche pan.

To make filling, arrange asparagus with ham in the pastry shell. In a separate bowl, beat eggs, then add flour. Add salt, paprika, milk and sour cream. Mix well. Pour over asparagus and ham, then sprinkle with extra grated cheese, if desired (again, 100 g gruyère and 25 g parmesan). Bake in a hot oven for 10 minutes, then reduce to moderate for 30–40 minutes.

The ham may be replaced with the
same quantity of prawns.

Tuna and silverbeet quiche

4 large leaves silverbeet, core removed
2 leeks or 1 onion, chopped
1 sheet frozen shortcrust pastry, thawed, or a purchased frozen
   shortcrust pie case
2 large eggs
½ cup cream or milk
Salt and pepper
95 g can tuna, drained
1 cup grated cheese
Grated cheese, extra

Wash silverbeet and chop well, adding some of the white stalks. Boil together with leeks in a little water for 5 minutes. Drain well and allow to cool. Grease a pie dish, line with pastry and bake in a moderate oven for 15 minutes. Beat eggs and cream with salt and pepper, then add tuna, cheese and silverbeet. Fill pastry case and top with more grated cheese. Bake in a moderate oven for 15 minutes or until set. Serve with salad.

Spinach quiche

3 eggs
1½ cups milk
1 cup grated cheese
1 small onion, diced
30 g butter, melted
½ cup self-raising flour, sifted
1 cup cooked spinach
Salt and pepper, to taste

Place all ingredients in a bowl and mix until well combined. Grease a 23 cm pie dish. Pour in mixture and bake in a moderate oven for approximately 1 hour.

Zucchini slice

3 bacon rashers or 4 slices ham
375 g grated unpeeled zucchini
1 large onion, finely chopped
1 cup grated cheddar cheese
1 cup self-raising flour, sifted
½ cup oil
5 eggs
Salt and pepper

Remove rind from bacon and chop finely. Combine zucchini, onion, bacon, cheese, flour, oil and lightly beaten eggs. Season with salt and pepper. Pour into a well-greased 20 x 30 cm lamington pan and bake in a 180° C oven for 30–40 minutes or until browned. Serves 4–6.

Vegetable and bacon quiche

BASE
4 tablespoons vegetable oil
4 tablespoons milk
1 cup self-raising flour

FILLING
1 medium grated carrot
1 medium zucchini
1 small onion
1 cup grated cheese
1 cup chopped bacon or ham (vegetarians can replace this with
  1 cup grated pumpkin or a finely chopped tomato; see Note)
3 eggs
¾ cup milk
¾ cup self-raising flour
½ teaspoon salt and pinch of pepper

For the base, mix together the oil and milk then stir into the flour. Press into the base and sides of a greased 23 x 4 cm quiche tin. Place the quiche on an oven tray in case the filling overflows. Preheat oven to 180°C.

For the filling, combine the vegetables, cheese and ham in a large bowl. In another bowl, combine the eggs, milk, flour, salt and pepper and add to the vegetables. Mix to combine. Pour into the prepared uncooked pastry base and bake for 40 minutes or until set.

Alternatively, place spoonfuls of base and filling mixture into a greased patty tin or mini muffin trays to make mini quiches for lunchboxes. Bake 10–15 minutes for patty cases and 15–20 minutes for mini muffin tins.

This makes eight good-sized meals served with vegetables or salads.

NOTE: If you have replaced the bacon with vegetables, the cooking time may need to be increased by 10–20 minutes.

Tuna, corn and onion quiche

4 eggs
1 cup low-fat milk
½ cup buttermilk
Pepper
½ cup self-raising flour
125 g tin sweetcorn kernels, drained
4 green onions, sliced
425 g tin tuna chunks in brine, well drained and flaked (substitute
* 450 g tin red or pink salmon if preferred)*
¾ cup low-fat grated tasty cheese
Baby rocket leaves and crusty bread, to serve

Preheat oven to 180°C. Lightly grease a 1.75 litre shallow quiche or baking dish. Whisk eggs, milk and buttermilk, season with pepper. Sift flour into bowl, stir through corn, onions, tuna and most of the cheese. Add egg mixture; mix well to combine. Pour into prepared dish, sprinkle with remaining cheese. Bake 35–40 minutes until set and golden. Cool slightly before cutting. Serve warm or cold with rocket and bread.

Impossible pie

¾ cup of pastry mix (if pastry mix is unavailable, use 125 g diced
    butter and ½ cup plain flour, rubbed in until well combined)
3 eggs
1 onion, chopped
1 small tin champignons, drained
2–3 rashers bacon, diced (pre-diced bacon may be used)
1 cup grated cheese
Salt and pepper
½ cup milk

Place the pastry mix (or the rubbed-in butter and flour) in a large bowl.
Add remaining ingredients and combine well. Pour into a greased pie dish
and bake at 180°C for 40–45 minutes.

Egg and bacon quiche

1 cup crushed plain savoury biscuits
1 cup grated carrot
1 cup grated cheese
1 cup chopped onion
4 bacon rashers, chopped
4 eggs, beaten
1 cup milk
Salt and pepper

Place biscuits, carrot, cheese, onion and bacon in a large bowl. Add eggs,
milk and salt and pepper to bowl. Mix well. Grease a quiche dish with
butter or oil and spoon mixture into it. Bake in a moderate oven until firm.
Serve with salad.

Olive and onion tart

2 cups plain (all-purpose) flour
100 g butter, chilled and cubed
4–5 tablespoons iced water
30 g butter, extra
1 kg onions, sliced
1 tablespoon French mustard
1 cup sour cream
3 eggs, lightly beaten
⅓ cup sliced black olives

Sift flour into bowl and rub butter into flour for 1 minute or until mixture is crumbly. Add almost all the water; mix to a firm dough, adding more water if necessary. Turn onto floured surface; knead 1 minute, then roll out to fit 23 cm flan tin. Press pastry into tin and refrigerate for 30 minutes.

Preheat oven to 180°C. Cut a sheet of baking paper to fit the flan tin; place over pastry and cover with dried beans or rice. Bake for 10 minutes, discard paper and beans; return pastry to oven for a further 10 minutes.

Heat extra butter in pan. Add onions, cook on low heat 45 minutes and allow to cool. Spread mustard over pastry. Whisk sour cream and eggs in a bowl. Spread onions over mustard and pour egg mixture over. Scatter olives on top. Bake 35 minutes or until filling has set. Stand 5 minutes before serving.

Chicken pie

PASTRY
2 cups plain flour
½ teaspoon salt
140 g butter
1 teaspoon water

FILLING
Pinch of pepper
2 tablespoons plain flour
½ teaspoon ground nutmeg
1 kg chicken thigh fillets, trimmed and cut into 2.5 cm cubes
2 large leeks, chopped
1 onion, thinly sliced
200 g ham, cut into 1 cm strips
75 g butter, melted
½ cup chicken stock
1 egg, beaten, for glazing,
½ cup cream

For the pastry, sift flour and salt into a bowl, rub in butter and add enough water to form a stiff dough. Knead lightly, then refrigerate. Preheat oven to 200°C. Grease a large shallow ovenproof dish with melted butter.

Combine pepper, flour and nutmeg in a plastic bag, toss chicken pieces in flour mixture until well coated. Shake off excess flour. Place half the leek and onion in layers over the base of prepared dish. Top with half the ham and chicken pieces. Repeat layers using remaining onion, leek, ham and chicken. Drizzle melted butter over filling, add stock.

Roll pastry to fit dish. Glaze edges of dish with a little egg. Cover pie with prepared pastry. Glaze with beaten egg. Cut three deep slits in the pastry to allow steam to escape — cream will be added through these later. Bake for 1 hour, or until pastry is golden brown and chicken is cooked. Remove from the oven and leave to stand for 5 minutes. Pour cream into slits and allow to stand for another 10 minutes before serving.

Spinach pie

500 g English spinach
1 tablespoon oil
6 spring onions (scallions), finely chopped
125 g feta cheese, crumbled
90 g grated cheddar cheese
5 eggs, lightly beaten
Salt and pepper
16 sheets frozen filo pastry, thawed
⅓ cup olive oil
1 egg, extra, lightly beaten, to glaze
1 tablespoon poppy seeds or sesame seeds

Preheat the oven to 210°C. Brush a 25 x 30 cm ovenproof dish with oil. Wash the spinach thoroughly and shred finely. Put in a large saucepan with just the water that is clinging to the leaves. Cook, covered, over low heat for 2 minutes, or until just wilted. Cool, wring out any excess water and spread out the shreds.

Heat the oil in a small frying pan and cook the spring onion for 3 minutes, or until soft. Transfer to a large bowl and add the spinach, cheeses and eggs then season. Stir until the cheeses are distributed evenly. Place one sheet of pastry in the dish, letting the edges overhang. Cover the remaining pastry with a clean, damp tea towel to prevent it from drying out. Brush the pastry in the dish with oil. Repeat with another seven layers of pastry, brushing each lightly with oil.

Spread the filling over the pastry, then fold in the edges of the pastry. Brush each remaining sheet of pastry lightly with oil and place on top of the pie. Tuck the edges down the sides, brush the top with egg and sprinkle with poppy seeds. Bake for 35–40 minutes, or until the pastry is golden. Serve immediately.

The younger set at a CWA ball, c1930

Main dishes

Beef and vegetable casserole (microwave)

2 tablespoons plain flour
500 g blade steak, cubed
2 carrots, sliced
2 potatoes, cubed
1 stalk celery, sliced diagonally
1 onion, sliced
450 g tin tomato soup
1 bay leaf
1 cup beef stock

Place flour and steak in a freezer bag, then shake to coat meat. Combine meat with all other ingredients in a microwave-safe casserole dish. Cook, uncovered, for 10 minutes on high. Stir, then cook for a further 45 minutes on medium, or until vegetables are tender. Stir and serve.

Oven-fried mustard chicken

1½ tablespoons dijon mustard
1 tablespoon lemon juice
½ teaspoon crumbled dried rosemary
3 large cloves garlic, minced
Pinch of pepper
6 chicken thighs or breasts, skinned
3 cups cornflakes, crushed
6 tablespoons parmesan cheese

Heat oven to moderately hot. Combine mustard, lemon juice, rosemary, garlic and pepper, then use to coat chicken. Combine cornflakes and cheese in a bag; shake chicken pieces to coat with the crumb mixture. Grease a baking dish and arrange chicken pieces in a single layer. Sprinkle remaining crumbs on top. Cover with foil and bake for 20 minutes. Remove foil and bake until juices run clear when chicken is pricked with fork.

Chicken in peanut sauce (microwave)

1 onion, finely chopped
1 garlic clove, crushed
30 g butter
¼ cup crunchy peanut butter
½ cup chicken stock
¼ cup honey
2 teaspoons mustard
1 teaspoon curry powder
Pinch cardamom
Dash Tabasco sauce
8 chicken thigh fillets
Rice, to serve

Combine onion, garlic and butter in a microwave-safe dish. Cook on high for 3 minutes. Stir in peanut butter, stock, honey, mustard, curry powder, cardamom and Tabasco sauce. Add chicken in a single layer. Cook on high for 6 minutes. Turn chicken over and cook for a further 6 minutes. Serve with rice.

Creamy beef stroganoff (microwave)

500 g rump steak
1 onion, thinly sliced
1 clove garlic, crushed
60 g butter
250 g mushrooms
¼ cup plain flour
1 cup beef stock
1 tablespoon dry sherry
1 tablespoon tomato sauce
1 teaspoon Worcestershire sauce
½ cup sour cream

Cut steak into fine strips. Combine onion, garlic and butter in a microwave dish, then cook on high for 3 minutes. Add mushrooms, then cook on high for 2 minutes. Toss steak in flour and add to dish with stock, sherry and the sauces. Cook on high for 5 minutes, reduce to medium high, then cook for 15 minutes or until meat is tender. Stir occasionally. Just before serving, stir in sour cream. Serve with rice or noodles.

Jumbuck stew

2 tablespoons flour
1 teaspoon salt, or to taste
1 teaspoon pepper
1 teaspoon curry powder
¼ teaspoon ground ginger
1 kg lamb shoulder chops
2 tablespoons oil
1 large onion, sliced
1 tablespoon brown vinegar
2 tablespoons tomato sauce
2 tablespoons Worcestershire sauce
1 tablespoon brown sugar
½ cup stock
500 g pumpkin, peeled and cut into large chunks

Combine flour, salt, pepper, curry powder and ginger and use to coat trimmed chops. Heat half the oil in a heavy pan and brown chops on each side. Transfer to a plate. Add remaining oil and cook onion until soft. Return chops to pan. Mix vinegar, sauces, sugar and stock together and pour over chops. Cover, simmer, then reduce heat to low and simmer gently for 1 hour. Skim any fat from surface. Add pumpkin to pan. Cover and cook a further 30 minutes or until chops are tender. Serve with hot herbed damper with chopped fresh herbs or mixed dried herbs added to the dough. Serves 6.

Meatloaf (microwave)

1 kg lean beef mince
1 onion, finely chopped
1½ cups wholemeal breadcrumbs
2 teaspoons mixed dried herbs
2 tablespoons tomato sauce
1 egg, beaten

Combine all ingredients. Press mixture into a 1.5 litre microwave loaf dish.
Cook on medium–high for approximately 15 minutes. Rotate dish halfway
through cooking. Stand, covered, for 5–10 minutes. The meat loaf is done
when it has shrunk slightly from the sides of the dish and the centre is still
moist. Drain off juices as they accumulate.

Meat patties (microwave)

500–600 g lean beef mince
½ onion, finely chopped
¾ cup wholemeal breadcrumbs
1 teaspoon mixed dried herbs
1 tablespoon tomato sauce
1 egg, beaten

Prepare patties or meatballs using half the ingredients of the Meatloaf
recipe (see above). Preheat a browning dish on high for 6 minutes, then
brush with oil. Quickly press both sides of patties firmly onto the base of
dish. Cook on high, allowing approximately 1½ minutes per patty. Stand
for 1–2 minutes.

Nora's fish dish (microwave)

1 large onion, sliced
1 tablespoon oil
Salt and pepper
1 tablespoon lemon juice
2 cups white sauce
500 g fish fillets
1 tablespoon chopped parsley
Breadcrumbs, for sprinkling
Parmesan cheese, for sprinkling

Cook onion in oil for 3 minutes. Add salt, pepper and lemon juice. Make a white sauce or use a prepared sauce mix and add to dish. Cut fish into pieces and cook separately for about 3 minutes on medium high or until just cooked. Add to dish of white sauce and stir in the parsley. Cover with a sprinkling of breadcrumbs and cheese and heat through. Serves 4.

Oriental beef and beans

500 g round steak
4 tablespoons oil
2 onions, cut into strips
250 g green beans, trimmed and cut into 5 cm pieces
1 cup sliced celery
½ cup sliced red and green capsicum
1½ tablespoons cornflour
1½ tablespoons soy sauce
1 cup beef stock
125 g fresh or 140 g tinned mushrooms, sliced

Trim fat from beef and slice steak finely into thin slices, 6–8 cm long. Heat oil in a frying pan and brown the steak quickly. Add onions, beans, celery and capsicum and cook for 5 minutes, stirring constantly. Blend cornflour with soy sauce and stock to make a smooth paste. Add mushrooms and paste to pan, stirring until the liquid is smooth. Reduce heat, cover pan and simmer until beans soften a little.

This dish is good served with Oriental Ginger and Cashew Rice (see page 104).

Pasta with bacon, tomato and olives

2 onions, chopped
3 cloves garlic, chopped
3 bacon rashers, chopped
2 x 400 g tins tomatoes, chopped
2 teaspoons tomato paste
½ teaspoon mixed dried Italian herbs
½ teaspoon sugar
Black olives
Salt and pepper
500 g pasta
250 g mozzarella cheese
Tasty cheese, grated

Fry onion, garlic and bacon in a little oil until onion is soft. Add tomatoes, tomato paste, herbs, sugar and olives. Simmer for 10 minutes. Season with salt and pepper.

Cook pasta until tender. Place cooked pasta mixed with mozzarella in an ovenproof dish and cover with sauce. Top with grated tasty cheese and cook in a moderate oven until cheeses melt. Serve alone or with tossed salad and Italian bread.

Pork in creamy prune sauce

500 g pork fillet
2 tablespoons plain flour
½ cup chopped prunes
½ cup white wine
1 tablespoon redcurrant jelly
300 ml cream
1 tablespoon lemon juice
1 cup chicken stock
Salt and pepper
2 tablespoons chopped parsley

Slice pork finely, toss in flour, then brown in a small amount of oil. Place in an ovenproof dish. Combine prunes and wine in a small pan and cook for 10 minutes. Add the prune and wine mixture, redcurrant jelly, cream, lemon juice and stock to the pork. Cook, covered, in a moderate oven for approximately 25 minutes or until pork is tender. Season to taste and serve sprinkled with parsley. Serves 4.

Potato moussaka

4 large potatoes
2 medium eggplants
Oil or butter, for frying
1 cup chopped onions
1 kg beef or lamb mince
2 cloves garlic
2 tablespoons Worcestershire sauce
800 g can tomatoes, drained
2 tablespoons sugar

TOPPING
3 eggs
¾ cup grated tasty cheese
¾ cup parmesan cheese
1 cup cream

Slice potatoes and eggplants fairly thinly. Fry in oil or butter until lightly browned and set aside.

Sauté the onions in a little butter, add meat, garlic and Worcestershire sauce and cook for 10 minutes, stirring often. Mash tomatoes with a fork and cook with sugar for 5 minutes, then combine with meat mixture. Grease a large casserole dish and line with some of the potato slices, cover with a layer of eggplant, then a layer of meat mixture, repeating layers until all mixture is used. Bake in a moderate oven for 45 minutes.

To make topping, beat eggs and combine cheeses and cream. Distribute over the moussaka and cook for a further 20 minutes until browned and firm.

Roast haunch of venison

1 venison roast
Melted butter
Salt and pepper
800 g plain flour
Port-flavoured gravy, to serve
Redcurrant jelly, to serve

Trim fat from meat. Brush meat with melted butter and season. Mix flour and enough water to make a stiff, lightly kneaded dough. Wrap around roast. Bake at 160°C for 25–30 minutes per 500 g for medium cooked, or 30–35 minutes for well done. When cooked, chip off pastry. Return meat to a very hot oven to brown. Serve with port-flavoured gravy and redcurrant jelly.

Veal with asparagus

1 kg veal forequarter
1 medium onion, diced
Butter or oil
2 cups chicken stock
4 large mushrooms, sliced
1 cup cooked asparagus pieces, fresh or tinned
1 cup white wine
Salt and pepper
Cornflour, to thicken
Rice, buttered noodles or couscous, to serve

Cut veal into 1½ cm cubes. Sauté onion in butter until golden, add veal and brown. Add chicken stock, simmer until tender. Add mushrooms, asparagus pieces and white wine. Season and thicken with cornflour. Serve with rice, buttered noodles or couscous. Serves 6.

Savoury beef pie

1 tablespoon shortening
250 g minced steak
1 tablespoon plain flour
1 tablespoon Worcestershire sauce
1 small carrot, finely chopped
¼ cup chopped celery (see Variation)
⅔ cup tomato juice or beef stock
½ teaspoon salt
1 onion, chopped
Shortcrust pastry (see Variation)

Place shortening in pan and when hot, brown meat slowly. Blend remaining ingredients together, add to meat and simmer, covered, until vegetables are almost tender. Place in a 20 cm pie dish and top with pastry. Seal edge of dish. Bake at 200–220°C for 20–30 minutes, or until golden brown.

VARIATION: May add ¼ cup peas to other vegetables.

Scone dough may be used for this pie instead of shortcrust pastry.

Stuffed chicken breasts

4 chicken breast fillets
4 thin slices ham
4 tablespoons grated cheese
4 large or 8 small asparagus spears
Plain flour
1 tablespoon oil
45 g butter
6 tablespoons Marsala
2 tablespoons chicken stock
Asparagus, extra, for garnishing

Flatten chicken between two pieces of plastic wrap, using a mallet or rolling pin. Place 1 slice of ham, 1 tablespoon of cheese and 1–2 asparagus spears on each fillet. Roll up and secure with toothpicks. Roll in flour.

Heat oil and 30 g butter in a frying pan, add chicken rolls and cook until tender, turning frequently. Remove toothpicks and place in a serving dish; keep warm. Add remaining butter, Marsala and stock to the pan. Bring to boil then simmer for a few minutes, stirring all the time. Spoon over chicken rolls and garnish with extra asparagus.

Tuna and mushroom sauce

90 g butter
1 large onion, finely chopped
450 g tin tuna in brine
90 g mushrooms
300 ml cream
2 tablespoons tomato paste
Salt and pepper
1 tablespoon chopped parsley
Ribbon pasta, to serve

Melt butter, add onion and cook gently until soft. Add tuna and mushrooms and stir over medium heat. Add cream, tomato paste and salt and pepper to taste. Bring to the boil, then remove immediately. Stir in parsley and serve over ribbon pasta.

Pastizzi

3 sheets ready-rolled puff pastry
400 g ricotta cheese
2 eggs
2 bacon rashers, chopped
½ cup frozen peas
Salt and pepper
Milk, to glaze

Thaw frozen pastry and cut into 23 cm squares. Dampen edges with water. With a fork, mix together remaining ingredients, except the milk. Place equal amounts of mixture in the centre of each square, raise corners of the pastry and seal edges to form a square envelope shape. Brush tops with milk. Bake at 180°C for 15–20 minutes until golden and crisp.

Barbecue meatloaf

500 g beef mince (see Note)
500 g pork mince
1 cup fresh breadcrumbs
2 onions, finely chopped
1 egg
1 teaspoon curry powder
1 tablespoon chopped parsley
Salt and pepper, to taste

BARBECUE SAUCE
½ cup brown sugar
1 scant teaspoon instant coffee
¼ cup Worcestershire sauce
½ cup tomato sauce
2 tablespoons vinegar
2 tablespoons lemon juice

For the meatloaf, combine minces, breadcrumbs, onion, egg, curry powder, parsley and salt and pepper in a bowl, mixing well. Form into a loaf shape and place on a baking tray. Bake in a moderate oven for 40 minutes.

For the sauce, combine all ingredients in a saucepan with ½ cup water, bring to boil, simmer for 5 minutes.

Pour the barbecue sauce over the meatloaf and cook for an additional 40 minutes, basting often. Serve hot with vegetables or cold with salad.

NOTE: To reduce the fat content of the dish, cook the meatloaf the day before, allow any fat to settle overnight then remove it before slicing or reheating to serve.

Cornish pastie

200 g beef mince
300 g potatoes, thinly sliced
200 g swede, thinly sliced
1 onion, very finely chopped (optional)
1 level teaspoon pepper
⅔ cup prepared or bought gravy
2 quantities hot water pastry (see below)
Milk, for brushing

Preheat oven to 200°C. Put the mince, potato, swede, onion and pepper into a large bowl, add gravy and stir well. Divide pastry into six portions and roll to 18 cm rounds. Place one sixth of mixture on one half of each round. Using a pastry brush, moisten all edges of pastry with milk then join and seal together by twisting with fingers (or press with a fork). Cut three slits on top of each pasty to allow steam to escape. Brush with milk. Put on a tray lined with baking paper.

Bake at 200°C for 20 minutes then turn the oven down to 185°C and bake for a further 20 minutes. Best eaten hot out of the oven with a side salad. Can be reheated.

Hot water pastry

½ cup sunflower oil
¼ cup boiling water
1½ cups self-raising flour
¼ teaspoon baking powder

Place all ingredients into a bowl and stir with a metal knife or spatula until well blended. Pat into a ball, wrap in plastic wrap or greaseproof paper and chill. When needed, divide into as many pieces as required. Roll out between two pieces of plastic wrap or greaseproof paper to make it easier to handle.

Chickpea and nut loaf

400 g tin chickpeas
1 tablespoon olive oil
1 finely chopped onion
2 cloves garlic, finely chopped
2 tablespoons tomato paste
1 teaspoon thyme leaves
200 g toasted unsalted mixed nuts
½ cup dry breadcrumbs
¼ cup chopped parsley
1 cup grated tasty cheese
2 beaten eggs
Salt and pepper, to taste

Preheat the oven to 180°C. Line a 20 x 12 x 6 cm loaf tin with baking paper, allowing it to overhang on two sides to allow for easy removal later. Rinse and drain the chickpeas and mash until smooth. Heat the oil in a frying pan over medium heat. Add the onion and garlic and cook for 5 minutes, then add the tomato paste and thyme and cook for a further 2 minutes.

Finely chop the nuts in a food processor. In a large bowl combine the onion mixture, nuts and remaining ingredients. Season well. Spoon the mixture into the prepared tin and bake for 30–35 minutes until firm and lightly golden. Remove from tin by lifting the baking paper.

This loaf is delicious served either hot with vegetables or cold with a garden salad.

Greek-style roast chicken

8 medium desiree potatoes, unpeeled
2 small brown onions or 1 large
1.4 kg free-range chicken
50 g butter, softened
3 garlic bulbs (1 bulb broken into cloves, and the other 2 bulbs
*   peeled and roughly chopped)*
8 sprigs thyme, roughly chopped
8 sprigs oregano, roughly chopped
1 lemon
200 ml extra virgin olive oil
Sea salt and pepper

Preheat oven to 240°C. Cook potatoes in a large pan of salted water for 25 minutes or until tender. Drain and set aside. Thickly slice the onions and place in base of a baking pan. Pat chicken dry with paper towel and trim wing tips. Slide fingertips underneath skin of breast and gently separate from flesh.

Mash together the butter, half of the chopped garlic and one third of the thyme and oregano. Push this mixture evenly under the skin of the chicken. Put one third of the remaining herbs and the remaining chopped garlic into the cavity. Halve the lemon and squeeze one half over the chicken. Put this squeezed lemon half into the chicken cavity. Slice the other lemon half into thin slices. Tuck a couple of slices between legs and breast, and put the rest over the chicken.

Put chicken in a baking dish. Scatter the unpeeled garlic cloves over chicken. Gently push down on potatoes with a masher and crush until skin splits. Arrange around chicken in baking dish. Drizzle chicken and potatoes with the olive oil and season with the salt and pepper. Scatter with the remaining herbs. Pour 50 ml water into dish and bake for 1 hour. Rest for 5–10 minutes. Serve with pan juices.

Macaroni and mince slice

MACARONI
1½ cups macaroni
30 g butter, melted
½ cup cream
2 eggs, lightly beaten
¾ cup grated tasty cheese
2 tablespoons grated parmesan cheese

MEAT SAUCE
60 g butter
1 clove garlic, crushed
1 onion, chopped
600 g beef mince
3 tablespoons tomato paste
2 teaspoons beef stock powder
Fresh parsley, to taste
Salt and pepper, to taste

CHEESE SAUCE
60 g butter
4 tablespoons plain flour
1½ cups milk
3 tablespoons grated tasty cheese
1 tablespoon chopped parsley
1 egg, lightly beaten

Cook the macaroni in a large saucepan of rapidly boiling water, uncovered, for 10 minutes or until just tender. Drain, then place in a 28 x 18 cm shallow ovenproof dish. Combine the remaining ingredients in a bowl and pour over macaroni.

For the meat sauce, heat the butter in a stainless steel or non-stick frying pan. Add the garlic and onion and cook, stirring, until onion is soft. Add mince and stir until well browned. Stir in the tomato paste, stock powder and ½ cup water. Reduce heat and simmer for 10 minutes, stirring occasionally. Add parsley and salt and pepper to taste. Spoon the meat sauce over the macaroni mixture.

For the cheese sauce, heat the butter in a small saucepan. Stir in the flour and cook, stirring, for 1 minute. Remove from heat and gradually add milk. Return to the heat, then stir until sauce boils and thickens, stirring occasionally. Add the cheese, parsley and egg and mix well.

Top the macaroni and meat sauce in the dish with the cheese sauce. Bake at 180°C for 30 minutes. Stand for 10 minutes before cutting into portions.

Chicken cacciatore

125 g button mushrooms
1 tablespoon oil
12 chicken drumsticks (about 1.2 kg)
1 medium onion, chopped
1 clove garlic, crushed
400 g tin tomatoes, puréed
½ cup white wine
½ cup chicken stock
1 teaspoon dried oregano
1 teaspoon dried thyme
Salt and pepper, to taste

Preheat oven to 180°C. Cut mushrooms into quarters. Heat oil in a heavy-based frying pan. Cook drumsticks in small batches over medium–high heat until well browned; transfer to a large ovenproof casserole dish.

Place the onion and garlic in a pan and cook over medium heat until golden. Spread over chicken. Add remaining ingredients to the pan and season to taste. Bring to the boil, reduce heat and simmer for 10 minutes. Pour mixture over chicken. Bake, covered, for 35 minutes or until chicken is very tender.

Piquant country beef with herb scones

1 kg chuck steak
¼ cup plain (all-purpose) flour
3 tablespoons oil
4 medium onions, roughly chopped
2 cloves garlic, crushed
⅓ cup plum jam
⅓ cup brown vinegar
1 cup beef stock
2 teaspoons sweet chilli sauce

HERB SCONES
2 cups self-raising flour
30 g butter
2 tablespoons chopped chives
2 tablespoons chopped parsley
¾ cup milk

Preheat the oven to 180°C. For the casserole, trim meat of excess fat and sinew and cut into 3 cm cubes. Toss in flour. Heat 2 tablespoons oil in a heavy-based pan. Cook meat quickly, in small batches, over medium–high heat until well browned. Drain meat on paper towel. Heat remaining oil in pan, add onion and garlic and cook, stirring, for 3 minutes or until soft. Combine onion mixture and meat in a large bowl. Add jam, vinegar, stock and chilli sauce, mix well. Transfer to an ovenproof dish. Cover and bake for 1½ hours or until meat is tender. Uncover dish, turn oven up to 240°C. Place herb scones on top of the meat and bake, uncovered, for 30 minutes or until scones are golden brown.

For the herb scones, sift flour into a bowl and rub in butter with fingertips until mixture resembles fine breadcrumbs. Stir in chives and parsley. Add milk; stir until just combined. Turn onto a lightly floured surface and knead until smooth. Press dough out to a 4 cm thick round. Using a pastry cutter, cut into 5 cm rounds.

NOTE: Casserole can be cooked 2 days ahead without the scones and refrigerated, or frozen for up to 2 weeks.

Veal chops with sage and lemon

4 veal loin chops
Plain flour, for dusting
1 egg, beaten
2 tablespoons milk
1 tablespoon finely chopped sage or
* 2 teaspoons dried sage*
¾ cup dried breadcrumbs
30 g butter
1 tablespoon olive oil
1 clove garlic, crushed
Lemon wedges, to serve

Trim excess fat from the veal chops, curl up tails of chops and secure in place with toothpicks.

Place the flour in a plastic bag. Place chops, one at at time, in the bag and coat thoroughly with flour; shake off any excess. Place egg and milk in a shallow bowl and stir to combine. Combine sage and breadcrumbs on a plate. Dip the floured chops in the egg mixture, then press lightly into the breadcrumb mixture, coating thoroughly.

Heat butter, oil and garlic in a large frying pan. Add chops in a single layer; fry on both sides over medium heat until cooked through. Serve with lemon wedges.

Lancashire hot pot

Butter or oil, for brushing
8 lamb forequarter chops, 2.5 cm thick
¼ cup plain flour
45 g butter
2 large brown onions, sliced
2 celery stalks, chopped
1 large parsnip, peeled and sliced
1¾ cups chicken or beef stock
200 g mushrooms, sliced
½ teaspoon white pepper
Salt, to taste
2 teaspoons dried mixed herbs
1 tablespoon Worcestershire sauce
4 medium old potatoes, very thinly sliced

Preheat the oven to 160°C. Brush a 1.5 litre capacity casserole dish with melted butter or oil. Trim meat of excess fat and sinew. Place flour in a plastic bag and toss chops in flour to coat thoroughly. Shake off excess and reserve for later use. Heat butter in a frying pan. Add chops and cook until both sides are brown. Remove chops and place in casserole dish.

Add onion, celery and parsnip to the pan; cook until slightly softened. Place mixture on top of chops in casserole dish.

Sprinkle reserved flour over base of pan and cook, stirring, until dark brown. Gradually pour in stock and stir until mixture comes to the boil. Add mushrooms, pepper, salt, herbs and Worcestershire sauce; simmer for 10 minutes. Remove from heat and pour over chops.

Place overlapping slices of potato on top to completely cover the meat and vegetables. Cover casserole dish with a lid and place in preheated oven. Cook for 1¼ hours. Remove the lid and cook for another 30 minutes or until potatoes are brown and crisp.

Pasta and vegetables

1 tablespoon olive oil
1 large onion, finely chopped
1 clove garlic, crushed
3 medium zucchini, sliced
4 button mushrooms, sliced
1 cup frozen peas
2 cups tomato pasta sauce
Salt and pepper, to taste
1 tablespoon oil, extra
1½ cups pasta (penne or spiralli)
⅓ cup grated parmesan cheese

Preheat oven to 150°C. Heat oil in a frying pan. Add onion and garlic and cook over low heat for 4 minutes or until onion is soft. Add zucchini and mushrooms and cook for 3 minutes. Add peas and pasta sauce and cook for another 3 minutes. Season, remove from heat and set aside.

Bring a large pan of water to a rapid boil. Add oil and pasta and cook for 10–12 minutes or until pasta is just tender. Drain and add to vegetables in pan, mixing well. Spoon mixture into a casserole dish. Sprinkle with parmesan cheese and bake, covered, for 20–30 minutes.

Mexican-style beef spare ribs

1.5 kg beef spareribs
2 bay leaves
¼ cup soft brown sugar
1 clove garlic, crushed

SAUCE
1 tablespoon vegetable oil
½ cup chopped onion
1 clove garlic, crushed
1 tablespoon sugar
2 tablespoons cider vinegar
425 g tin tomato purée
1 tablespoon Mexican-style chilli powder, or to taste
1 teaspoon dried oregano
1 teaspoon ground cumin
Hot pepper sauce, to taste

Place ribs and bay leaves in a large pan. Combine brown sugar and garlic with 1½ cups water and pour over ribs. Heat until boiling, then reduce heat, cover and simmer gently, turning ribs occasionally, until tender, 30–45 minutes.

For the sauce, heat the oil in a small pan, add onion and garlic and cook until soft. Stir in sugar, vinegar, purée, chilli powder, oregano, cumin and pepper sauce. Heat until boiling, reduce heat and simmer, stirring occasionally, for 5 minutes. Cover and keep warm.

Drain ribs and pat dry on paper towel. Grill about 13 cm above glowing coals, turning and basting frequently with sauce, for 10–15 minutes. Serve with remaining sauce.

Veal with wine and mustard sauce

6 veal steaks, about 140 g each
½ cup plain flour
1 teaspoon ground mustard seeds
45 g butter
2 teaspoons oil
1 cup good-quality white wine
⅔ cup chicken stock
3 teaspoons seeded mustard

Trim meat of fat and sinew. Combine the flour and mustard seeds on a sheet of baking paper. Toss meat in the seasoned flour; shake off excess. Reserve 3 teaspoons of seasoned flour.

Heat the butter and oil in a large heavy-based frying pan. Add the steaks to the pan. (Unless you have a very large pan you will have to cook them in batches.) Cook the meat over medium–high heat for 3–4 minutes each side. Remove from pan, drain on paper towel and keep warm. Repeat with remaining steaks.

Add the combined wine, stock, mustard and reserved seasoned flour to the pan, stirring to incorporate any browned bits from the bottom. Stir until the mixture boils and thickens. Divide veal among serving plates and pour the sauce over.

Eggplant parmigiana

1.5 kg eggplants
Salt, for sprinkling
Plain flour, seasoned with salt and pepper
350 ml olive oil
500 ml tomato passata or tomato pasta sauce
2 tablespoons roughly torn basil leaves
250 g mozzarella cheese, chopped
1 cup grated parmesan cheese

Thinly slice the eggplant lengthways. Layer the slices in a large colander, sprinkling salt between each layer. Leave for 1 hour to degorge. Rinse and pat the slices dry on both sides with paper towel, then coat lightly with the seasoned flour.

Preheat the oven to 180°C and grease a shallow 2.5 litre baking dish.

Heat 125 ml of the olive oil in a large frying pan. Quickly fry the eggplant slices in batches over high heat until crisp and golden on both sides. Add more olive oil as needed and drain the slices on paper towel as you remove each batch from the pan.

Make a slightly overlapping layer of eggplant slices over the base of the dish. Season with pepper and a little salt. Spoon 4 tablespoons of passata over the eggplant and scatter some of the basil over the top. Sprinkle with some mozzarella, followed by some parmesan. Continue layering until you have used up all the ingredients, finishing with a layer of the cheeses.

Bake for 30 minutes. Remove from the oven and allow to cool for 30 minutes before serving. Serves 8.

Chicken casserole with olives and tomato

1 tablespoon olive oil
1 large onion, chopped
2 garlic cloves, crushed
8 pieces chicken, skin on
1 tablespoon tomato paste
1½ cups white wine
Pinch of sugar
8 large ripe tomatoes, chopped
4 tablespoons parsley, chopped
180 g green beans, trimmed and halved
130 g olives
Salt and pepper

Heat the oil in a large flameproof casserole and fry the onion for a minute or two. Add the garlic and the chicken and fry for as long as it takes to brown the chicken all over.

Add the tomato paste and white wine, along with the sugar, and stir everything together. Add the tomato and any juices, the parsley and the beans and bring to the boil. Turn down the heat, season well and simmer for 40 minutes.

Add the olives and simmer for another 5 minutes. The sauce should have thickened and the chicken should be fully cooked. Add salt and pepper, if necessary. Serve with potatoes.

Pork chops pizzaiola

4 pork chops
4 tablespoons olive oil
Salt and pepper
600 g ripe tomatoes
3 garlic cloves, crushed
3 basil leaves, torn
1 teaspoon finely chopped parsley

Using scissors or a knife, cut the pork fat at 5 mm intervals around the rind. Brush the chops with 1 tablespoon of the olive oil and season well.

Remove the stems from the tomatoes and score a cross in the bottom of each one. Blanch in boiling water for 30 seconds. Transfer to cold water, peel the skin away from the cross and chop the tomatoes.

Heat 2 tablespoons of the oil in a saucepan over low heat and add the garlic. Soften without browning for 1–2 minutes, then add the tomato and season. Increase the heat, bring to the boil and cook for 5 minutes until thick. Stir in the basil.

Heat the remaining oil in a large frying pan with a tight-fitting lid. Brown the chops in batches over medium–high heat for 2 minutes on each side. Place in a slightly overlapping row down the centre of the pan and spoon the sauce over the top, covering the chops completely. Cover the pan and cook over low heat for about 5 minutes. Sprinkle with parsley to serve.

Fish and cumin kebabs

750 g skinless firm white fish fillets
2 tablespoons olive oil
1 garlic clove, crushed
3 tablespoons chopped coriander leaves
2 teaspoons ground cumin
1 teaspoon pepper

Cut the fish fillets into 3 cm cubes. Thread on oiled skewers and set aside.

To make the marinade, combine the oil, garlic, coriander, cumin and pepper in a small bowl. Brush the marinade over the fish, cover with plastic wrap and refrigerate for several hours, or overnight, turning occasionally. Drain, reserving the marinade. Season just before cooking.

Put the skewers on a hot, lightly oiled barbecue flatplate. Cook for 5–6 minutes, or until tender, turning once and brushing with reserved marinade several times during cooking.

Suitable fish for this dish are blue-eye, snapper or perch.

Chicken and asparagus stir-fry

2 tablespoons oil
1 garlic clove, crushed
10 cm piece fresh ginger, peeled and thinly sliced
3 boneless, skinless chicken breasts, sliced
4 spring onions, sliced, plus extra finely shredded spring onion,
   to garnish
200 g asparagus spears, cut into short lengths
2 tablespoons soy sauce
30 g slivered almonds, roasted

Heat a wok over high heat, add the oil and swirl to coat the side. Add the garlic, ginger and chicken and stir-fry in batches for 1–2 minutes, or until the chicken changes colour.

Add the spring onion and asparagus and stir-fry for a further 2 minutes, or until the spring onion is soft.

Stir in the soy sauce and 60 ml water, cover and simmer for 2 minutes, or until the chicken is tender and the vegetables are slightly crisp. Sprinkle with the almonds and serve at once, topped with shredded spring onion.

Slow-cooked shanks

1 tablespoon oil
4 lamb shanks
2 red onions, sliced
10 cloves garlic, peeled
400 g tin chopped tomatoes
½ cup dry white wine
1 bay leaf
1 teaspoon grated lemon zest
1 large red capsicum, chopped
Salt and pepper
3 tablespoons chopped parsley

Preheat the oven to 170°C. Heat the oil in a large flameproof casserole dish, add the shanks in batches and cook over high heat until browned on all sides. Return all the lamb to the casserole.

Add the onion and garlic to the casserole and cook until softened. Add the tomato, wine, bay leaf, lemon zest, capsicum and ½ cup water and bring to the boil.

Cover the casserole and cook in the oven for 2–2½ hours, or until the meat is tender and falling off the bone and the sauce has thickened. Season to taste. Sprinkle the parsley over the top before serving. Serve with couscous or soft polenta.

Rosemary-infused lamb and lentil casserole

1 tablespoon olive oil
1 onion, finely sliced
2 cloves garlic, crushed
1 small carrot, finely chopped
2 teaspoons cumin seeds
¼ teaspoon chilli flakes
2 teaspoons finely chopped fresh ginger
1 kg boned leg of lamb, cut into 4 cm cubes
2 teaspoons rosemary leaves, chopped
3 cups chicken stock
1 cup green or brown lentils
3 teaspoons soft brown sugar
2 teaspoons balsamic vinegar
Salt and pepper

Preheat the oven to 180°C. Heat half the oil in a large, heavy-based pan. Add the onion, garlic and carrot and cook over medium heat for about 5 minutes, or until soft and golden. Add the cumin seeds, chilli flakes and ginger, cook for 1 minute, then transfer to a large casserole dish.

Heat the remaining oil in the pan and brown the lamb in batches over high heat. Transfer to the casserole.

Add the rosemary to the pan and stir in 2½ cups of the stock. Heat until the stock is bubbling, then pour into the casserole dish. Cover the dish and bake for 1 hour.

Add the lentils, sugar and vinegar and cook for 1 hour more, or until the lentils are cooked. If the mixture is too thick, stir in the remaining stock. Season with salt and pepper to taste and serve.

Prawn curry

1 tablespoon butter
1 onion, finely chopped
1 clove garlic, crushed
1½ tablespoons curry powder
2 tablespoons plain flour
2 cups skim milk
1 kg raw prawns, peeled and deveined
1½ tablespoons lemon juice
2 teaspoons sherry
1 tablespoon finely chopped parsley
Rice, to serve

Heat the butter in a large saucepan. Add the onion and garlic and cook for 5 minutes, or until softened. Add the curry powder and cook for 1 minute, then stir in the flour and cook for a further 1 minute.

Remove from heat and stir in the milk until smooth. Return to a low heat and stir constantly until the sauce has thickened. Simmer for 2 minutes and then stir in the prawns. Continue to simmer for 5 minutes, or until the prawns are just cooked.

Stir in the lemon juice, sherry and parsley and serve immediately with rice.

CWA Dunedoo branch

Salads
and
vegetable sides

Boxing day salad

DRESSING
½ cup mayonnaise
1 tablespoon lemon juice

500 g cooked turkey, diced
4 stalks celery, chopped
4 shallots, chopped
½ cup chopped nuts
½ red capsicum

To make dressing, blend mayonnaise and lemon juice. Combine all other ingredients then stir dressing through. Other seasonings may be added to the dressing, if desired.

Potato bacon salad

2 kg washed new potatoes, unpeeled
250 g rindless bacon
Small bunch chives, chopped

DRESSING
300 ml sour cream
2 tablespoons vinegar
2 tablespoons milk, optional

If potatoes are small, cook whole, and if large, cut into bite-sized pieces. Do not overcook. Rinse under cold water. Drain and cool. Chop bacon and fry until golden, drain and cool.

To make dressing, mix ingredients until smooth. Combine with bacon and chives and pour over potatoes, mixing gently.

Curried vegetable pasta salad

500 g pasta shells or spirals
1 large carrot
1 small zucchini
¼ red capsicum
300 g broccoli, chopped
1 shallot, chopped
200 g button mushrooms, thickly sliced

DRESSING
1 small onion, chopped
Crushed garlic, to taste
1 teaspoon curry powder
Pinch turmeric
⅓ cup mustard pickles
½ cup low-fat mayonnaise
½ cup low-fat sour cream

To make the salad, boil the pasta and keep warm. Cut the carrot, zucchini and capsicum into long strips. Add the carrot and broccoli to boiling water and half-cook. Drain and combine all vegetables, including shallot and mushrooms, with the pasta.

To make the dressing, heat a pan and add the onion, garlic, curry, turmeric, pickles and 5 tablespoons water. Cook until onion softens. Combine mayonnaise and sour cream in a bowl, then add mixture to pan. Stir until the sauce thickens. Pour over pasta and vegetables and serve.

Seafood salad and sauce

500 g cooked prawns, peeled and deveined
150 g mixed lettuce leaves
2 large avocados, thinly sliced

DRESSING
¼ cup mayonnaise
¼ cup tomato sauce
¼ cup lightly whipped cream
¼ teaspoon curry powder
1 teaspoon lemon juice
1 teaspoon Worcestershire sauce
Salt and pepper, to taste

Combine prawns, lettuce and avocado. Combine all dressing ingredients and mix well. Drizzle salad with prepared dressing.

Zucchini salad

500 g zucchini, diced
½ small red onion, finely chopped
1 medium tomato, finely diced
2–3 tablespoons basil leaves
1 tablespoon red wine vinegar
1 tablespoon oil
1 tablespoon lemon juice
Salt and pepper, to taste

Simmer zucchini for 2–3 minutes. Drain and cool. Combine with all other ingredients and toss gently.

Spinach salad with dreamy creamy dressing

2 large bunches English spinach
4 bacon rashers, trimmed
4 eggs, boiled
12 button mushrooms

DRESSING
½ cup mayonnaise
1 teaspoon sugar
1 teaspoon mustard
1 clove garlic
3 tablespoons lemon juice
½ cup sour cream
2 spring onions, including tops
1 tablespoon dried parsley
Salt and pepper, to taste

To make the salad, wash the spinach and chop finely. Cook the bacon until crisp; drain, allow to cool and chop finely. Coarsely chop the eggs. Clean and slice the mushrooms. Place all ingredients into a large salad bowl and refrigerate until ready to serve. Pour dressing over the salad and toss.

To make the dressing, place all ingredients in a blender and blend until the mixture is smooth. Refrigerate until ready to use. Dressing makes 1½ cups.

Bacon and avocado salad

8 rindless bacon rashers
400 g green beans, trimmed and halved
300 g baby English spinach leaves
2 French shallots, finely sliced
2 avocados

DRESSING
¼ teaspoon brown sugar
1 clove garlic, crushed
⅓ cup olive oil
1 tablespoon balsamic vinegar
1 teaspoon sesame oil
Salt and pepper

Preheat the grill. Put the bacon on a tray and grill on both sides until it is nice and crisp. Leave it to cool and then break into pieces.

Bring a saucepan of water to the boil and cook the beans for 4 minutes. Drain, then hold them under cold running water for a few seconds to stop them cooking any further.

Put the spinach in a large bowl and add the beans, bacon and shallots. Halve the avocados, then cut into cubes and add them to the bowl.

To make the dressing, mix the brown sugar and garlic in a small bowl. Add the rest of the ingredients and whisk everything together.

Pour the dressing over the salad and toss well. Grind some black pepper over the top and sprinkle with some salt.

Cannellini bean salad

425 g tin cannellini beans
1 tomato, finely chopped
3 anchovy fillets, sliced
1 tablespoon finely chopped red onion
2 teaspoons finely chopped basil
2 teaspoons extra virgin olive oil
1 teaspoon balsamic vinegar
Crusty bread, cut into slices, to serve
Olive oil, for brushing
1 garlic clove, bruised

Rinse and drain the cannellini beans. Combine the cannellini beans, tomato, anchovies, onion, basil, olive oil and balsamic vinegar.

Lightly brush the slices of bread with the oil, then toast and rub with the garlic. Spoon the salad onto the bread slices to serve.

Roast tomato salad

6 roma tomatoes
2 teaspoons capers
6 basil leaves, torn
1 tablespoon olive oil
1 tablespoon balsamic vinegar
2 garlic cloves, crushed
½ teaspoon honey
Salt and pepper

Cut the tomatoes into quarters lengthways. Cook, skin side down, on a hot barbecue grill plate or flat plate or under a kitchen grill for 4–5 minutes, or until golden. Cool to room temperature.

Combine the capers, basil, oil, vinegar, garlic and honey in a bowl, season with salt and pepper to taste, and pour over the tomatoes. Toss gently and serve immediately.

Baked pumpkin casserole

1 kg pumpkin
1 heaped tablespoon plain flour
2 eggs, beaten
4 tablespoons milk
Salt and freshly ground black pepper
60 g grated cheese

Chop pumpkin into pieces, boil until tender, then mash. Sift flour, add eggs, milk and seasoning. Add pumpkin and cheese. Bake in a casserole dish, uncovered, in a moderate oven for 20–25 minutes.

Braised cabbage

1 onion
¼ cup bacon
1 teaspoon butter
3–4 cups shredded cabbage
Salt and pepper, to taste
1 tablespoon boiling water

Chop onion and bacon and lightly fry in butter. Add cabbage, salt and pepper. Add boiling water and cook gently for 10 minutes, stirring occasionally.

VARIATION: Add 2 teaspoons curry powder to 1 tablespoon boiling water and 1 tablespoon melted butter. Stir in chopped cabbage and cook for 5–10 minutes, stirring occasionally.

Potato casserole (microwave)

3 large potatoes, sliced
3 bacon rashers, chopped
1 large onion, sliced
1½ cups grated tasty cheese
¾ cup cream
Paprika
30 g butter

In a well-greased microwave-safe casserole dish, place potato, bacon, onion and cheese in layers, repeating layers until all ingredients are used. Boil cream, then pour over potatoes. Sprinkle paprika on top and add a couple of small knobs of butter. Microwave on medium–high for 20 minutes.

Potatoes romanoff

6 large potatoes (about 1.5 kg), peeled
600 g sour cream
8 shallots, chopped
125 g grated cheese, plus extra for sprinkling
Salt and pepper
Paprika

Cook potatoes until just tender, drain and cool. Coarsely grate potatoes into a large bowl. Add sour cream, shallots, grated cheese and salt and pepper. Place in a greased casserole dish; top with extra grated cheese and sprinkle with paprika. Cover and refrigerate overnight. Bake, uncovered, in a moderate oven for 45–50 minutes.

Grated potato cakes

3 large potatoes
1 small onion, grated
½ cup grated cheese
1 egg, lightly beaten
1 tablespoon plain flour
1 tablespoon wholegrain mustard
1 tablespoon chopped parsley
1 teaspoon powdered chicken stock
Salt and pepper, to taste
2 tablespoons oil, for shallow-frying

Peel and grate potatoes coarsely, squeeze out any excess moisture and dry between sheets of paper towel. Place all ingredients, except for the oil, in a bowl and mix thoroughly. Heat oil in a non-stick frying pan over medium heat and drop ¼ cups of mixture into oil (3 or 4 at a time). Flatten slightly and cook until brown on both sides. Not suitable to microwave or freeze.

Zucchini bake

600 g zucchini, trimmed and grated (to give 4 cups)
4 eggs, beaten
¼ cup plain flour, sifted
½ cup grated cheese, plus extra for sprinkling
1 teaspoon salt
3 tablespoons chopped parsley
3 tablespoons sliced spring onion
1 clove garlic, crushed
¼ teaspoon pepper
1 punnet cherry tomatoes

Using paper towel, squeeze out as much moisture as possible from the zucchini. In a bowl, combine eggs, flour, cheese, salt, parsley, onion, garlic and pepper. Stir in zucchini and place mixture in a greased shallow baking dish. Cut tomatoes in half and place in dish with the cut side facing up. Sprinkle extra cheese over tomatoes, if desired. Bake, uncovered, at 180° C for 30 minutes or until mixture is set.

Zucchini with garlic butter

500 g zucchini
60 g butter
1 clove garlic, crushed
½ teaspoon salt
Pepper, to taste

Wash zucchini, remove ends, but do not peel. Shred coarsely. Melt butter, add garlic and stir for a few seconds. Add the zucchini and seasoning and toss in the butter for 4 minutes. Serve immediately.

Spinach and orange salad

10 to 12 medium English spinach leaves
4 oranges, peeled
1 medium red onion, peeled and sliced thinly
½ cup pitted black olives, drained
¼ cup toasted pine nuts
⅓ cup olive oil
¼ cup red wine vinegar

Wash and dry spinach leaves. Remove large stems. Tear into bite-sized pieces. Segment oranges by carefully removing all white pith, leaving each segment bare of any skin at all. Add onion, olives and pine nuts. Whisk together olive oil and vinegar till well combined. Pour dressing over salad and toss well. Best served as soon as possible.

Curried potato

6 large potatoes
1 large onion, chopped
1 tablespoon extra virgin olive oil
1 teaspoon curry powder, to taste
300 ml thickened cream

Peel potatoes and cut into 1 cm slices. Sauté onion in olive oil over medium heat until translucent. Remove from oil. Return oil to the heat and add curry powder. Quickly cook curry powder without burning it. Add cream and onion and remove from heat. Place potato slices in the bottom of a baking dish and pour over the cream mixture, making sure the mixture covers all pieces. Cook at 180°C for 25 minutes or until potato is tender. Increase the heat for the last 5 minutes, to brown the top.

Moroccan eggplant

3–4 eggplants
1 kg roma tomatoes
3–4 teaspoons ground cumin
3–4 teaspoons ground coriander
3–4 teaspoons paprika
6–8 cloves garlic
1 bunch flat-leaf (Italian) parsley
Olive oil
½ cup red wine vinegar
Salt and freshly ground black pepper
¼ cup sundried tomatoes, chopped

Slice eggplants, spray slices with oil, then roast or grill. Season roma tomatoes and roast for 15 minutes at 200°C. Put spices on a tray lined with baking paper and toast in the oven for 5–8 minutes. Roughly chop garlic and parsley. Whisk oil and vinegar together and season. Combine eggplant slices, tomatoes, sundried tomatoes, spices and parsley (or you could use a mint and garlic mixture). Dress with vinaigrette and adjust seasoning.

Honey-glazed carrots (microwave)

500 g carrots, finely diced
2 tablespoons honey
2 tablespoons orange juice
Pinch salt
1 tablespoon butter
2 tablespoons vinegar
2 teaspoons cornflour

Place carrots in a microwave-safe bowl with 1 tablespoon water. Microwave on high, covered, for 7 minutes, or less if more crisp carrots are preferred. Drain. Combine all other ingredients and microwave on high for 1 minute. Stir. Pour over carrots and microwave on high for 2 minutes.

Oriental ginger and cashew rice (microwave)

1 cup long-grain rice
2 cups hot water
30 g butter
1 clove garlic
½ cup raw cashews, chopped
¼ cup chopped glacé ginger
1 teaspoon grated lemon rind
¼ teaspoon ground cumin
2 tablespoons chopped mint

Combine rice and water in a large, shallow microwave-safe dish. Cook on high for 15 minutes, stirring occasionally. Combine butter, garlic and nuts in a dish and cook on high for 2 minutes. Stir. Combine rice, nut mixture and remaining ingredients; cook on high for about 3 minutes or until heated through, stir occasionally. Serves 4–6.

Tomato and capsicum stew

2 tablespoons olive oil
1 large red onion, chopped
2 large red capsicums, chopped
1 large green capsicum, chopped
4 large ripe tomatoes, peeled and chopped
2 teaspoons soft brown sugar

Heat oil in medium pan, add onion and cook over low heat until it is soft. Add capsicums and cook over medium heat for 5 minutes, stirring constantly. Stir in tomato and brown sugar. Reduce heat, cover and cook for 6–8 minutes or until vegetables are tender.

Tomato pumpkin

¼ pumpkin
1 medium onion
3 tablespoons tomato paste
2 cloves garlic, chopped
Salt and pepper, to taste
1 tablespoon olive oil, or to taste

Peel pumpkin and cut into 2 cm squares. Finely dice onion. Place cut pumpkin and onion into a baking dish and mix together with tomato paste, garlic, salt and pepper. Add olive oil and combine well. Bake in a moderate oven for about 30 minutes, stirring occasionally, until the pumpkin is just tender.

Vegetable slice

400 g mixed vegetables, roughly chopped (see Variation)
1 medium onion
1 cup grated tasty cheese
2 slices ham (optional)
1 cup self-raising flour, sifted
Salt and pepper, to taste
½ cup oil
4 eggs

Mix vegetables, onion, cheese, ham (if using), sifted flour and salt and pepper together. Add oil and eggs, lightly beaten. Line a slice pan with baking paper. Spoon mixture into pan and cook in a moderate oven for 30–40 minutes.

VARIATION: May use a packet of mixed chopped Chinese vegetables. Alternatively, this dish can be made with a single vegetable.

Asparagus stir-fried with mustard

480 g asparagus (see Variation)
1 tablespoon oil
1 red onion, sliced
1 garlic clove, crushed
1 tablespoon wholegrain mustard
1 teaspoon honey
125 ml cream

Break the woody ends off asparagus. Cut asparagus into 5 cm lengths.

Heat the wok until very hot, add the oil and swirl to coat the sides.
Stir-fry the onion for 2–3 minutes, or until tender. Stir in the crushed garlic
and cook for 1 minute. Add the asparagus to the wok and stir-fry for
3–4 minutes, or until tender, being careful not to overcook the asparagus.

Remove the asparagus from the wok, set it aside and keep it warm.
Combine the wholegrain mustard, honey and cream. Add to the wok and
bring to the boil, then reduce the heat and simmer for 2–3 minutes, or until
the mixture reduces and thickens slightly. Return the asparagus to the wok
and toss it through the cream mixture. Serve immediately.

VARIATION: When asparagus is in season, white and purple asparagus
are also available. Vary the recipe by using a mixture of the three colours.
Do not overcook the purple asparagus or it will turn green.

This dish can also be served on croutons,
toasted ciabatta or toasted wholegrain bread
as a smart appetiser or first course.

Vegetables with honey and soy

1 tablespoon sesame seeds
1 tablespoon oil
1 teaspoon sesame oil
1 garlic clove, crushed
2 teaspoons grated fresh ginger
2 spring onions, thinly sliced
250 g broccoli, cut into small florets
1 red capsicum, thinly sliced
1 green capsicum, thinly sliced
150 g button mushrooms, halved
30 g pitted black olives, halved
1 tablespoon soy sauce
1 tablespoon honey
1 tablespoon sweet chilli sauce

Place the sesame seeds on an oven tray and toast under a hot grill for a couple of minutes, or until golden. Heat a wok, add the oils and swirl to coat the base and side of the wok. Add the garlic, ginger and spring onion and stir-fry for 1 minute.

Add the broccoli, capsicums, mushrooms and olives to the wok. Stir-fry for a further 2 minutes, or until the vegetables are just tender.

Combine the soy sauce, honey and chilli sauce in a bowl. Pour over the vegetables and then toss lightly. Sprinkle with the toasted sesame seeds and serve immediately.

Tricolour pasta salad

2 tablespoons olive oil, plus 1 tablespoon extra
2 tablespoons white wine vinegar
1 small clove garlic, halved
375 g tricolour pasta spirals
¾ cup sundried tomatoes in oil, drained
½ cup pitted black olives
100 g parmesan cheese
1 cup quartered artichoke hearts
½ cup shredded fresh basil leaves

Combine olive oil, vinegar and garlic in a small screw-top jar. Shake well then allow to stand for 1 hour.

Bring a large saucepan of water to the boil. Slowly add the pasta spirals and cook until just tender. Drain then toss with the extra olive oil while still hot. Allow to cool completely.

Cut sundried tomatoes into fine strips and cut olives in half. Shave parmesan cheese into paper-thin slices.

Place pasta, tomato, olives, cheese, artichokes and basil in a large serving bowl. Remove garlic halves from dressing and discard. Pour the dressing over the salad. Toss gently to combine.

Green beans with tomato and olive oil

⅓ cup olive oil
1 large onion, chopped
3 cloves garlic, finely chopped
400 g tin diced tomatoes
½ teaspoon sugar
750 g green beans, trimmed
3 tablespoons chopped parsley

Heat the oil in a large frying pan, add onion and cook over medium heat for 4–5 minutes, or until softened. Add the garlic and cook for a further 30 seconds.

Add ½ cup water, the tomato and sugar and season to taste. Bring to the boil, then reduce the heat and simmer for 10 minutes, or until reduced slightly. Add the beans and parsley and simmer for a further 10 minutes, or until the beans are tender and the tomato mixture is pulpy. Season with salt and pepper to taste and serve immediately.

Gunnedah younger set, photographed at Frances Studdy Rest Home

Desserts

Apple pie

FILLING
6 green apples (about 1 kg), peeled and chopped
½ cup sugar
Juice of ½ lemon

PASTRY
125 g butter
½ cup caster sugar
1 egg
200 g plain flour
100 g self-raising flour

Stew apples with sugar, lemon juice and enough water to prevent sticking. Cool. For the pastry, beat butter and caster sugar; add egg and combine well. Add flours. Using fingers, press two-thirds of the mixture into a greased 20 x 30 cm lamington tin. Pour apple into uncooked pastry case; coarsely grate the remainder of the rolled-out pastry over the apple. Bake in a moderate oven for 30 minutes or until golden.

Baked apple pudding

60 g butter
¾ cup caster sugar
1 egg
Good pinch ground cloves
1 cup self-raising flour, sifted
¼ teaspoon bicarbonate of soda (baking soda)
3 cups thinly sliced apples

Cream butter and sugar. Combine with egg and cloves, then sifted flour and bicarbonate of soda. Add apples and mix well. Spoon into a greased baking dish and bake in a moderate oven for 50–60 minutes.

Khoshaf (dried fruit salad)

500 g dried apricots
250 g prunes
125 g raisins (see Variation)
125 g blanched almonds, halved
60 g pistachio nuts or pine nuts
125–250 g caster sugar, to taste
1 tablespoon rose water
1 tablespoon orange flower water

Wash fruits and place into a large bowl. Mix with nuts and cover with water. Add sugar and sprinkle with rose water and orange flower water (available from pharmacies or health food stores). Allow to stand for at least 48 hours. This allows the syrup to become rich with the juices of the fruit and the salad to acquire a golden colour.

VARIATION: Add 125 g of dried figs and dried peaches.

Bread and butter pudding

30 g butter, softened
6 thin slices day-old white or brown bread, crusts removed
¾ cup mixed dried fruit
3 tablespoons caster sugar
1 teaspoon mixed spice
2 eggs, lightly beaten
1 teaspoon vanilla essence
2½ cups milk

Preheat oven to 180°C. Grease a medium-sized shallow ovenproof dish. Butter bread on one side and cut slices in half diagonally. Layer bread into the dish, sprinkling each layer with dried fruit, sugar and spice.

Beat the eggs, essence and milk together. Pour mixture over the bread and set aside for 5 minutes to soak. Bake pudding for 50 minutes, or until it is set and the top is browned.

Mascarpone and lime torte

200 g packet ginger biscuits
50 g butter
2 limes
500 g mascarpone cheese
40 g icing sugar, sifted
50 g dark chocolate
Grapes, to garnish (optional)
50 g caster sugar (optional)

Grease an 18 cm springform cake tin and line the side with baking paper. Mix together crushed biscuits and melted butter. Press into the base of the tin. Finely zest the limes, then juice them. Place mascarpone, icing sugar, lime zest and juice in a bowl and beat together. Spread over biscuit base and chill for 30 minutes.

To decorate, grate chocolate over the top. If garnishing with grapes, dip grapes in water, shake off excess water, dip into caster sugar then arrange on torte. Serves 6–8.

For variety, use orange or lemon instead of lime. Alternatively, decorate the torte with lime, lemon or orange slices.

Pavlova roll

Cornflour, for dusting
4 egg whites
¾ cup caster sugar, plus 1 tablespoon extra
1 teaspoon cinnamon
½ cup slivered almonds

FILLING
300 ml thickened cream, whipped
Grated chocolate, to taste

Grease and line a 26 x 32 cm Swiss roll tin, then dust with cornflour. Beat egg whites until stiff, gradually adding caster sugar to form a meringue. Spread meringue mixture into prepared tin. Sprinkle combined sugar, cinnamon and almonds over meringue. Bake in a moderate to moderately hot oven for 7–10 minutes, or until firm and golden-tipped. Turn out onto baking paper resting on a cake cooler. Cool for at least 5 minutes.

Beat cream until stiff, then fold in grated chocolate. Carefully spread over meringue. Trim edges, then roll up from the long side like a Swiss roll. Refrigerate until set. Decorate with confectionery, if desired, and more grated chocolate.

VARIATION: Spread roll with strawberry jam, then lightly cover with cream. Top with fresh halved strawberries and roll up. Decorate with whole strawberries.

Buttermilk pannacotta

20 g powdered gelatine
2½ cups cream
220 g caster sugar
400 ml buttermilk
2 teaspoons vanilla essence
Raspberry sauce, to serve

Sprinkle gelatine over ¼ cup water in a small heatproof bowl then place over a saucepan of simmering water and stir until gelatine has dissolved. Combine cream, sugar and buttermilk in another pan and heat gently until sugar has dissolved.

Remove from heat and stir in vanilla and gelatine until well combined. Pour into six 200 ml moulds rinsed out with cold water and chill, covered, for 4 hours or overnight, until set.

Turn pannacotta onto chilled plates. Serve with raspberry sauce or the sauce of your choice.

Apricot layer parfait

8 macaroons or small meringues
2 tablespoons sherry
400 g tin apricot halves, drained (see Variation)
⅔ cup whipped cream

Place 2 tablespoons of crushed macaroons in each of four dessert glasses. Sprinkle with a little sherry and spoon in a layer of chilled, drained apricot halves. Place 1 large tablespoon whipped cream on apricots. Repeat layers until all apricots are used and glass is filled.

VARIATION: Use 250 g strawberries instead of apricots.

Brown sugar tart

SWEET COFFEE PASTRY
100 g caster sugar
180 g butter, chilled
300 g plain flour
½ cup cold coffee

FILLING
400 g brown sugar
1 teaspoon cornflour
4 eggs, beaten
100 ml cream
1 teaspoon vanilla essence
100 g melted butter

For the pastry, combine caster sugar, butter and flour in a food processor, and pulse into fine crumbs. Add coffee and bring together into a pliable dough. Wrap and chill for 30 minutes.

Roll pastry to fit a 30 cm loose-bottomed flan tin, trim and chill. Blind bake in a moderately hot oven for 10 minutes. Allow to cool before filling.

For the filling, combine sugar and cornflour, stir in eggs and mix well, followed by cream, vanilla and melted butter. Mix well.

Pour into tart case and bake in a low oven for about 1 hour or until custard is just set. Chill before serving with poached fruit.

Ice cream cake

375 g mixed fruit
½ cup brandy
1 madeira cake (about 450 g)
4 litres vanilla ice cream
125 g dark chocolate chips
Strawberries or 100 g packet glacé cherries, to decorate

Line two 10 x 22 x 8 cm deep loaf tins with foil or baking paper. Chop fruit and sprinkle with approximately 3 tablespoons brandy. Cut cake into cubes and sprinkle with remaining brandy. Soften ice cream and mix half of it with fruit, cake and chocolate chips. Spoon one quarter of the plain vanilla ice cream into each tin, pressing firmly and smoothing the top. Top each plain layer with half of the combined ice cream, cake and fruit mixture, pressing firmly and smoothing as before. Divide the remaining plain ice cream between the two tins and smooth the top.

Cover with foil or baking paper. Freeze until firm, preferably overnight. Remove from freezer 10–15 minutes before serving. Turn onto oblong platters. Decorate with cut strawberries or cherries. Each loaf serves about 10–12 when sliced. Any leftover mixture can be frozen separately for another occasion.

This recipe makes a generous quantity, so is handy for a party or large gathering.

Butterscotch self-saucing pudding

Oil or butter, for brushing
90 g butter, softened
1 cup soft brown sugar
1½ cups self-raising flour, sifted
1 teaspoon mixed spice
¾ cup milk
60 g butter, extra
½ cup sugar

Preheat oven to 180°C. Brush six 1-cup capacity ovenproof dishes with oil or melted butter. Using electric beaters, beat butter and sugar in a small mixing bowl until light and creamy. Transfer to a large mixing bowl. Using a metal spoon, fold in flour and mixed spice alternately with milk. Spoon evenly into dishes. Place on a baking tray.

Place extra butter, sugar and ¼ cup water in a small pan. Stir over low heat until butter has melted and sugar has dissolved. Bring to boil, reduce heat and simmer gently, uncovered, until golden brown. Remove from heat. Very carefully stir in 1 cup water. Stir over low heat until smooth; allow to cool slightly.

Pour an equal amount of butterscotch mixture over each pudding. Bake for 35 minutes, or until a skewer inserted halfway into the centre of the pudding comes out clean. Loosen each pudding by running a knife around the edge. Invert onto serving plates.

Baked rice custard

Melted butter or oil, for brushing
¼ cup short-grain rice
2 eggs
¼ cup caster (superfine) sugar
1½ cups milk
½ cup cream
1 teaspoon vanilla extract
1–2 teaspoons grated lemon zest
¼ cup sultanas or currants (optional)
¼ teaspoon ground cinnamon or nutmeg

Preheat the oven to 160°C. Brush a deep 20 cm round ovenproof dish with melted butter or oil. Cook rice in a medium pan of boiling water until just tender and drain.

In a medium bowl, whisk the eggs, sugar, milk, cream, vanilla and zest for about 2 minutes. Fold in the cooked rice and sultanas or currants, if using. Pour mixture into prepared dish. Sprinkle with nutmeg or cinnamon.

Place filled dish into a deep baking dish. Pour in water to come halfway up the side of the baking dish. Bake for 50 minutes or until custard is set and a knife comes out clean when inserted in the centre. Remove the dish from the baking dish immediately. Allow to stand for 5 minutes before serving. Serve with cream or stewed fruits.

Passionfruit mousse

5–6 passionfruit
6 eggs, separated
185 g caster sugar
½ teaspoon finely grated lemon zest
3 tablespoons lemon juice
1 tablespoon gelatine
315 ml cream, lightly whipped
40 g flaked coconut, toasted

Cut the passionfruit in half and scoop out the pulp. Strain, reserving the seeds and pulp, then measure out 3 tablespoons juice and set aside. Add the seeds and pulp to the remaining juice and set aside. Put the egg yolks, 125 g of the sugar, the lemon zest, lemon juice and strained passionfruit juice in a heatproof bowl. Put the bowl over a saucepan of simmering water and, using electric beaters, beat for 10 minutes, or until thick and creamy. Remove from the heat and transfer to a glass bowl.

Sprinkle the gelatine over 125 ml water in a small bowl and leave until spongy. Put the bowl in a pan of just-boiled water (the water should come halfway up the side of the bowl) and stir until dissolved. Add the gelatine to the mousse mixture and mix well. Mix in the passionfruit pulp and leave until cold, then fold in the whipped cream.

Using electric beaters, whisk the egg whites until soft peaks form. Gradually whisk in the remaining sugar, beating until it has dissolved. Fold the egg whites into the mousse mixture quickly and lightly. Spoon into eight 250 ml ramekins or stemmed wine glasses. Refrigerate for 2 hours, or until set. Sprinkle with the coconut just before serving.

Mango and passionfruit pies

750 g ready-made sweet shortcrust pastry
3 mangoes, peeled and sliced or chopped,
* or 400 g tinned mango slices, drained*
60 g passionfruit pulp, strained
1 tablespoon custard powder
90 g caster sugar
1 egg, lightly beaten
Icing sugar, to dust
Cream, to serve

Preheat the oven to 190°C. Grease six 10 x 8 x 3 cm fluted flan tins or round pie dishes. Roll out two-thirds of the pastry between two sheets of baking paper to a thickness of 3 mm. Cut out six 13 cm circles, line the tins with them and trim the edges. Refrigerate while you make the filling.

Combine the mango, passionfruit, custard powder and sugar in a bowl.

Roll out the remaining pastry, including the trimmings, between two sheets of baking paper to 3 mm thick. Cut out six 11 cm circles. Re-roll the pastry trimmings and cut into shapes for decoration.

Fill the pastry cases with the mango mixture and brush the edges with egg. Top with the pastry circles and press the edges to seal. Trim the edges and decorate with the pastry shapes. Brush the tops with beaten egg and dust with icing sugar.

Bake for 20–25 minutes, or until golden brown. Serve with cream.

Lemon delicious

70 g unsalted butter, at room temperature
185 g sugar
2 teaspoons finely grated lemon zest
3 eggs, separated
30 g self-raising flour
185 ml milk
4 tablespoons lemon juice
Icing sugar, to dust
Thick cream, to serve

Preheat the oven to 180°C. Melt 10 g of the butter and use to lightly grease a 1.25 litre ovenproof ceramic dish.

Using electric beaters, beat the remaining butter, the sugar and grated zest together in a bowl until light and creamy. Gradually add the egg yolks, beating well after each addition. Fold in the flour and milk alternately to make a smooth but runny batter. Stir in the lemon juice.

In another bowl, whisk the egg whites until firm peaks form and, with a large metal spoon, fold one-third of the whites into the batter. Gently fold in the remaining egg whites, being careful not to overmix.

Pour the batter into the prepared dish and place in a large roasting tin. Pour enough hot water into the tin to come one-third of the way up the side of the roasting tin. Bake for 55 minutes, or until the top of the pudding is golden, risen and firm to the touch. Leave for 5 minutes before serving. Dust with icing sugar and serve with cream.

Peach pie

500 g ready-made sweet shortcrust pastry
1.65 kg tinned peach slices, well drained
125 g caster (superfine) sugar
30 g cornflour (cornstarch)
¼ teaspoon almond essence
20 g unsalted butter, chopped
1 tablespoon milk
1 egg, lightly beaten
Caster sugar, for sprinkling

Roll out two-thirds of the dough between two sheets of baking paper until large enough to line a 23 x 18 x 3 cm pie dish. Remove the top sheet of paper and invert the pastry into the dish. Use a small ball of pastry to press the pastry into the dish. Trim any excess pastry with a knife. Refrigerate for 20 minutes.

Preheat the oven to 200°C. Line the pastry with crumpled baking paper and pour in baking beads or rice. Bake for 10 minutes, remove the paper and beads and return to the oven for 5 minutes, or until the pastry base is dry and lightly coloured. Allow to cool.

Mix the peaches, sugar, cornflour and almond essence in a bowl, then spoon into the pastry shell. Dot with butter and moisten edges of the pastry with milk.

Roll out the remaining dough to a 25 cm square. Using a fluted pastry cutter, cut into ten strips 2.5 cm wide. Lay the strips in a lattice pattern over the filling, pressing firmly on the edges, and trim. Brush with egg and sprinkle with sugar. Bake for 10 minutes, reduce the heat to 180°C and bake for 30 minutes more, or until golden. Cool before serving.

Grandmother's pavlova

4 egg whites
Pinch salt
230 g caster sugar
2 teaspoons cornflour
1 teaspoon white vinegar
500 ml cream
3 passionfruit, to decorate
Strawberries, to decorate

Preheat oven to 160°C. Line a 32 x 28 cm baking tray with baking paper.

Place the egg whites and salt in a dry bowl. Using electric beaters, beat until stiff peaks form. Add the sugar gradually, beating constantly after each addition, until mixture is thick and glossy and all sugar is dissolved.

Using a metal spoon, fold in the cornflour and vinegar. Spoon the mixture into a mound on the prepared tray. Lightly flatten the top of the pavlova and smooth the sides. (This pavlova should have a cake shape and be about 2.5 cm high.) Bake for 1 hour, or until pale cream in colour and crisp. Remove from the oven while warm and carefully turn upside down onto a plate. Allow to cool.

Lightly whip the cream until soft peaks form and spread over the soft centre of the pavlova. Decorate with passionfruit pulp and halved strawberries. Cut into wedges to serve.

Self-saucing chocolate pudding

Melted butter, for brushing
1 cup self-raising flour
3 tablespoons cocoa powder
½ cup caster sugar
1 egg
½ cup milk
60 g butter, melted
1 teaspoon vanilla essence
1 cup soft brown sugar
1½ cups boiling water
Whipped cream or ice-cream, to serve

Preheat the oven to 180°C. Brush a 2-litre heatproof dish with melted butter. Sift the flour and 1 tablespoon cocoa into a large bowl and add the sugar. Make a well in the mixture.

Beat the egg in a jug and add the milk, melted butter and vanilla essence. Pour the liquid into the dry ingredients and, using a wooden spoon, stir the batter until it is well combined and lump free. Pour into the prepared dish.

Combine the brown sugar and the remaining cocoa and sprinkle evenly over the batter. Pour the boiling water gently and evenly over the ingredients in the dish. Bake for 30–40 minutes, or until the pudding is cooked—a sauce will have formed underneath. Serve hot with whipped cream or ice cream.

For a crunchy alternative, add half a cup of chopped walnuts to the pudding batter before baking.

Rhubarb and pear crumble

600 g rhubarb
2 strips lemon zest
1 tablespoon honey, or to taste
2 firm, ripe pears
½ cup rolled oats
¼ cup wholemeal plain flour
⅓ cup soft brown sugar
50 g butter

Trim the rhubarb, wash and cut into 3 cm pieces. Place in a medium pan with the lemon zest and 1 tablespoon water. Cook, covered, over low heat for 10 minutes, or until tender. Cool a little. Stir in the honey and remove the lemon zest.

Preheat the oven to 180°C. Peel and core the pears and cut into 2 cm cubes. Combine with the rhubarb. Pour into a 1.25 litre dish and smooth the surface.

To make the topping, combine the oats, flour and brown sugar in a bowl. Rub in the butter with your fingertips until the mixture is crumbly. Spread over the fruit. Bake for 15 minutes, or until cooked and golden.

Cherry strudel

470 g tin or jar pitted cherries, drained
¾ cup very finely chopped walnuts
½ cup caster sugar
1 tablespoon grated lemon zest
1 teaspoon ground cinnamon
1 teaspoon ground allspice
¾ cup fresh white breadcrumbs
¼ cup melted butter, plus extra for brushing
1 sheet frozen puff pastry, thawed
Poppy seeds, for sprinkling (optional)
Whipped cream, for serving

Halve cherries and set aside in a colander to drain. Combine walnuts, sugar, zest, cinnamon and allspice in a large bowl.

In another bowl, combine breadcrumbs and butter. Add breadcrumb mixture to nut mixture; stir well.

Lay the sheet of pastry on a work surface and brush with a little melted butter. Spread with breadcrumb mixture, then cherries, leaving a 5 cm margin on each side. Fold over lengthways and press edges together firmly. Tuck in short ends. Brush all over with melted butter and sprinkle with poppy seeds if using. Place on a greased oven tray and bake for 10 minutes in a hot oven, then reduce heat to moderate and bake for a further 25–30 minutes or until golden. Serve warm with whipped cream.

Mango fool

3 large mangoes
1 cup custard
1⅔ cups cream
Fresh fruit, to serve (optional)

Peel and stone mangoes and purée the flesh in a food processor. Add the custard and blend to combine.

Whip cream until soft peaks form, then gently fold into the mango mixture until just combined. Do not overmix, as you want to end up with a marbled effect.

Pour the mixture into a serving dish or six individual glasses. Gently smooth the top, then refrigerate for at least 1 hour before serving. Serve with fresh fruit if desired.

Evans Head 10th birthday, 4 November 1939

Cakes
and
muffins

Date loaf

  1 teaspoon bicarbonate of soda
  1 cup boiling water
  1 cup chopped dates
  1 tablespoon butter, softened
  ¾ cup brown sugar
  1 egg, lightly beaten
  1½ cups plain flour, sifted
  1 teaspoon cinnamon

Mix bicarbonate of soda in boiling water and add to dates in a bowl. Allow to cool. Cream butter and brown sugar, then add egg and prepared date mixture. Stir in flour and cinnamon. Place mixture in a greased and lined loaf tin and bake in a moderate oven for approximately 1 hour.

Pumpkin loaf

  2 tablespoons butter, softened
  ¾ cup caster sugar
  1 teaspoon vanilla essence
  1 cup cold mashed pumpkin
  2 cups self-raising flour, sifted
  Pinch salt
  ¾ cup milk
  2 tablespoons chopped walnuts
  1 cup sultanas

Mix butter and sugar, then add vanilla and pumpkin. Fold in sifted flour, salt, milk, nuts and sultanas. Mix well. Bake in a well-greased and lightly floured 20 x 12 x 7 cm loaf tin or 2 smaller tins in a moderate oven on centre shelf for 30–45 minutes depending on size of tin. Serve cold, sliced and buttered.

Irene's date and walnut loaf

1 tablespoon butter, softened
1 cup brown sugar
1 egg
1 cup chopped dates
1 teaspoon bicarbonate of soda
1 cup boiling water
140 g chopped walnuts
2 cups plain flour, sifted
1 teaspoon baking powder

Mix together butter and brown sugar, then add egg. Over medium heat, beat together dates, bicarbonate of soda and water until thick. Add walnuts. Combine with butter mixture, along with sifted flour and baking powder. Bake in a greased and lined loaf tin in a moderate oven for approximately 1 hour. Slice and spread with butter.

Fruit loaf

1 cup cold tea
1 cup sugar (brown or white)
1 cup mixed dried fruit
2 cups self-raising flour, sifted

Soak together tea, sugar and fruit for 2 hours. Fold in sifted flour. Bake in a greased and lined bar cake tin in a moderate oven for 40–50 minutes.

Angel food cake

4 large egg whites
½ teaspoon cream of tartar
Vanilla
⅔ cup caster sugar
¼ cup plain flour
1 tablespoon cornflour
Pinch salt
Whipped cream, to serve
Strawberries, to serve

Dust a deep 20 cm ring tin with flour or line bottom with baking paper; do not grease. Beat egg whites until foamy, add cream of tartar, beat until very stiff, then add a little vanilla. Sift together sugar, flour and cornflour. Carefully fold all dry ingredients, 2 tablespoonfuls at a time, into the egg whites. Spoon the mixture into the tin and bake in a moderate oven for about 25 minutes. Remove from oven and leave in the tin until cold. Cover with whipped cream and strawberries.

Chocolate cake

125 g butter, softened
1 cup caster sugar
2 eggs
170 g self-raising flour
2 tablespoons cocoa
½ cup milk
¼ teaspoon vanilla
2 tablespoons boiling water

Cream butter and sugar. Add eggs and beat well after each addition. Sift the flour and cocoa together. Fold half the sifted flour and cocoa into the creamed mixture, then the milk and vanilla, then the remaining sifted flour mixture. Stir in boiling water last. Bake in a greased and lined deep 17 cm round cake tin or a square tin in a moderate oven for 40–45 minutes.

Banana blueberry cake

125 g butter, softened
1 cup caster sugar
1 teaspoon vanilla
2 eggs
2 cups self-raising flour, sifted
⅓ cup sour cream or thick yoghurt
1 cup mashed bananas
½ cup blueberries

Place butter, sugar and vanilla in a bowl and beat until light and creamy. Add eggs and beat well. Fold through sifted flour, sour cream, mashed bananas and finally whole blueberries, making sure not to crush them. Spoon the mixture into a 22 cm greased and lined round cake tin and bake in a preheated moderate oven for 1 hour or until cooked. Allow to cool in tin before turning out.

Banana cake

125 g butter, softened
¾ cup caster sugar
2 eggs
1½ cups plain flour
1 teaspoon baking powder
Pinch salt
3 ripe bananas, mashed and sprinkled with 1 teaspoon lemon juice
6 dates, chopped (optional)

Cream together butter and sugar, then add eggs, one at a time, and beat well. Sift flour, baking powder and salt. Add a little of the flour mixture to the creamed mixture before adding bananas and lemon juice. Add remaining flour and dates, if using. Bake in a greased and lined deep 20 cm ring tin in a moderate oven for 35–40 minutes.

Banana sponge

4 eggs, separated
¾ cup caster sugar
2 ripe bananas, well mashed
½ cup cornflour
¾ cup plain flour
1 teaspoon cream of tartar
Pinch salt
½ teaspoon bicarbonate of soda
4 tablespoons hot water
Whipped cream, to fill

Beat egg whites in a medium bowl until stiff, gradually add sugar and beat for 5 minutes. Add egg yolks and bananas and beat for 1 minute. Fold in well-sifted flours, cream of tartar and salt. Fold in bicarbonate of soda dissolved in hot water. Pour into two greased and lined 22 cm round sandwich tins and bake in a moderate oven for 25 minutes. Turn out onto wire racks to cool, then sandwich cakes with whipped cream.

Basic butter cake

125 g butter, softened
1 cup caster sugar
1½ cups self-raising flour, sifted
½ teaspoon salt
2 eggs
A little more than 1 cup milk

In a bowl, beat all ingredients at medium speed for 4 minutes. Bake in a greased and lined 20 cm round cake tin at 180°C for 40–45 minutes.

VARIATIONS: Orange cake – Add grated zest of 1 orange. **Chocolate cake** – Replace 2 rounded tablespoons of flour with same quantity of cocoa. **Base for lamingtons** – Bake in a square cake tin or lamington tin.

Beetroot cake

250 g butter, softened
1 cup caster sugar
4 eggs
250 g fresh beetroot
150 g currants
2 teaspoons grated lemon zest
1 tablespoon lemon juice
1 cup plain flour
1 cup self-raising flour
½ teaspoon nutmeg

Grease a 14 x 21 cm loaf tin and line the base with paper. Cream butter and sugar until light and fluffy. Beat in eggs one at a time. Add peeled and finely chopped beetroot, currants, lemon zest and juice and half of the flours sifted with the nutmeg. Mix well. Stir in remaining sifted flours. Spread mixture in the prepared tin. Bake in a moderate oven for about 1½ hours or until cooked. Allow to stand for 5 minutes before turning out to cool.

Pumpkin muffins

2 cups self-raising flour, sifted
¼ teaspoon cinnamon
¼ teaspoon nutmeg
½ teaspoon bicarbonate of soda
¼ cup brown sugar
¼ cup chopped raisins
1 egg
½ cup milk
¼ cup oil
1 cup mashed pumpkin

Mix all dry ingredients in a bowl. Add egg, milk, oil and pumpkin. Mix in lightly. Bake in greased muffin tins in a moderate oven for 25–30 minutes.

Carrot and sultana cake

2 eggs
¾ cup caster sugar
¾ cup oil
½ teaspoon vanilla
1 teaspoon bicarbonate of soda
½ teaspoon mixed spice
½ teaspoon salt
1 cup plain flour
1½ cups finely grated carrots, lightly packed
½ cup sultanas and/or ½ cup chopped walnuts

Combine eggs, sugar, oil and vanilla, then sift in dry ingredients. Beat at a low speed until smooth. Stir in carrots, sultanas and/or walnuts. Mix well and pour mixture into a greased and lined 20 x 10 x 7 cm loaf tin. Bake in a moderate oven for 40–45 minutes.

Crunchy coffee cake

125 g butter
½ cup sugar
2 eggs
1¼ cups self-raising flour, sifted
3 tablespoons milk
½ teaspoon vanilla

TOPPING
4 tablespoons self-raising flour
2 tablespoons melted butter
2 teaspoons cinnamon
1 tablespoon desiccated coconut
2 tablespoons brown sugar

Cream butter and sugar until light, then add well beaten eggs. Fold in sifted flour alternately with milk and vanilla. Spoon into a greased and lined deep 20 cm round tin.

For topping, sift flour and combine with other ingredients and sprinkle over mixture. Bake in a moderate oven for 45 minutes.

Chocolate macaroon cake

MACAROON
1 egg white
Pinch salt
½ cup caster sugar
2 cups desiccated coconut
1 tablespoon plain flour
¼ cup chopped walnuts

CAKE
125 g butter, softened
1 cup caster sugar
2 eggs
2 cups self-raising flour
2 tablespoons cocoa
1 cup milk
1 teaspoon vanilla

ICING
2 cups icing sugar
1 heaped tablespoon cocoa
35 g butter, softened
Milk, to mix
Walnuts, to decorate

To make the macaroon, beat egg white with salt until mixture holds its shape. Beat in sugar. Mix coconut with plain flour and mix into egg white mixture. If the mixture is crumbly, add 1 tablespoon water. Add walnuts and divide mixture into two equal portions.

To make cake, cream butter and sugar until light and fluffy. Add eggs one at a time and mix through. Sift flour and cocoa together and add about one-third of the creamed mixture. Add one-third of the combined milk and vanilla and continue adding, alternating ingredients until combined.

Grease a deep 20 cm round tin. Spoon one-third of cake mixture into the tin, spreading evenly, then half the macaroon mixture, then another third of cake mixture, the rest of the macaroon mixture and then the remaining cake mixture. Bake in a moderate oven for 1 hour or until cooked when tested with a skewer.

To make the icing, sift the icing sugar and cocoa, then mix in butter and milk until consistency is easy to spread. Decorate the iced cake with chopped walnuts.

Chocolate ripple cake

125 g butter, softened
¾ cup caster sugar
2 eggs
1½ cups self-raising flour
⅔ cup milk

RIPPLE MIXTURE
1 tablespoon cocoa
¼ cup caster sugar
⅓ cup chopped walnuts
½ tablespoon butter

Cream butter and sugar, add eggs and beat well. Sift flour and add alternately with milk. Spoon half the mixture into a greased and lined 20 cm ring tin. Combine ripple mixture ingredients and then crumble over the cake mixture into the tin. Place remaining cake mixture on top. Bake in a moderate oven for 35 minutes or until cooked. Ice with chocolate ganache or as desired.

Dutch cake

3 tablespoons butter, softened
½ cup caster sugar
1 egg
¼ cup self-raising flour
1 teaspoon mixed spice
1 teaspoon cinnamon
¼ teaspoon nutmeg
¼ cup desiccated coconut
¼ cup mixed fruit
¼ cup chopped nuts
½ cup milk

Cream butter and sugar, then beat in egg. Sift together dry ingredients and fold in with coconut, fruit, nuts and milk. Pour into a greased and lined 18 cm cake tin and bake in moderate oven for 30–40 minutes. Ice with lemon icing (see below).

Lemon icing

2 tablespoons milk, at room temperature, plus extra as needed
2 teaspoons lemon juice
2 teaspoons butter, softened
200 g icing sugar
1 teaspoon grated lemon rind

Combine milk, lemon juice, butter and sifted icing sugar and beat well. Add lemon zest last. Add more icing sugar or more milk, to thicken or thin if needed.

Fruit cake

1 kg mixed dried fruit
100 g glacé cherries
75 g walnuts
⅓ cup rum
250 g butter, softened
250 g brown sugar
5 eggs
1 teaspoon vanilla essence
1 tablespoon golden syrup
340 g plain flour
1 small teaspoon baking powder
1 teaspoon cinnamon
1 teaspoon mixed spice

Combine dried fruit, cherries, walnuts and rum, cover and leave overnight. Prepare a 22 cm round or square cake tin. Grease tin and line with several layers of newspaper and two layers of baking paper. Cream butter and sugar. Add eggs one at a time, beating well after each addition. Add essence and golden syrup. Sift dry ingredients. Add dry ingredients alternately with fruit to creamed mixture. Spoon mixture into the prepared tin. Bake in a low oven for 1 hour, then reduce to a very low oven for 2 hours.

Ginger sponge

¾ cup caster sugar
5 eggs
1 tablespoon golden syrup
⅓ cup self-raising flour
⅓ cup cornflour
3 teaspoons ground ginger
1 teaspoon ground cinnamon
2 teaspoons cocoa

ICING
125 g butter, softened
250 g icing sugar
2 teaspoons boiling water

Beat the sugar and eggs for 8 minutes or until mixture holds its shape. Add golden syrup and beat through to combine. Sift dry ingredients together three times. Add dry mixture to the liquid mixture and stir to combine. Bake in two greased and lined 22 cm sandwich tins in a moderate oven for 20 minutes. Do not open the oven door during that time.

To make buttercream icing, beat butter until smooth. Gradually add the icing sugar, mixing well, then add the water and mix well.

Honey roll

4 eggs
110 g brown sugar
60 g caster sugar, plus extra for sprinkling
2 teaspoons honey
140 g self-raising flour
½ teaspoon cinnamon
¼ teaspoon bicarbonate of soda
15 g cornflour
1 teaspoon butter
2 tablespoons hot water
Mock cream (see below) or whipped cream

Beat eggs in a medium bowl until thick, add sugars slowly and beat until light and thick. While beating, add honey. Sift dry ingredients several times and fold in lightly. Melt butter in hot water and fold in. Prepare a swiss roll tin and line with baking paper. Pour mixture into the tin and bake in a moderate oven for about 25 minutes. Do not overcook, as this mixture burns easily. Turn out onto paper or cloth sprinkled with caster sugar. Trim edges and carefully roll up tightly. When cooled, unroll and fill with mock or whipped cream, then reroll.

Mock cream

2 cups sugar
120 g butter
½ teaspoon vanilla

Heat sugar and ⅓ cup water in a saucepan, stirring constantly over heat until sugar is dissolved. Increase heat and bring to the boil. Remove from heat and allow to cool completely. Beat butter and vanilla until white and fluffy, then gradually pour in cold syrup, beating constantly. Refrigerate until ready for use. If cream should separate while refrigerated, allow the mixture to return to room temperature, then beat well until reconstituted.

Kentish cake

170 g butter, softened
¾ cup caster sugar
2 eggs
1 cup self-raising flour
2 tablespoons desiccated coconut
2 tablespoons cocoa
¼ cup milk
90 g sultanas, nuts and cherries

Cream butter and sugar, then add eggs, beating well after each addition.
Fold in sifted dry ingredients, add the milk, fruit and nuts. Bake in a deep
greased and lined 20 cm round cake tin or a 14 x 21 cm loaf tin for
45 minutes, or until cooked. Turn out onto a wire rack to cool then ice
with caramel or chocolate icing.

Norwegian sour cream cake

2 eggs
2 cups caster sugar
2 cups sour cream
3 cups plain flour
1 teaspoon bicarbonate of soda
½ teaspoon cinnamon
½ teaspoon cardamom
2 or 3 drops almond essence

Beat eggs and sugar until creamy, then add sour cream and well-sifted
dry ingredients in alternate lots. Add almond essence. Blend well. Grease
a 24 cm ring tin and line with baking paper. Pour mixture into tin and
bake in a moderate oven for 55–60 minutes. When cooked, leave in tin
for 10 minutes before turning out. Serve plain or spread with butter.

Lemon tea cake

1½ cups plain flour
¼ teaspoon salt
1 teaspoon baking powder
1 cup caster sugar
125 g butter, chilled and cubed
2 eggs, beaten
½ cup milk
Grated zest and juice of 1 lemon
½ cup chopped walnuts
¼ cup sugar, extra

Grease a 20 cm ring tin and line base with baking paper. Sift flour, salt and baking powder into a bowl. Add sugar. Rub in the butter until it resembles fine breadcrumbs, or use a food processor to achieve this result. Combine eggs and milk, stir into mixture, then fold in lemon zest and walnuts. Spoon mixture into the tin and bake in a moderate oven for about 1 hour. Mix the lemon juice and extra sugar in a cup and pour over cake as soon as it is removed from the oven. Allow to cool in tin.

Macaroon cake

115 g butter, softened
115 g caster sugar
3 egg yolks
½ cup milk
1 teaspoon vanilla
180 g self-raising flour, sifted

TOPPING
3 egg whites
115 g caster sugar
115 g desiccated coconut

Cream butter and sugar, then add egg yolks and beat. Add milk, vanilla and sifted flour and stir well. Place in a well-greased and lined 20 x 30 cm lamington tin or rectangular slice tin.

To make topping, beat egg whites until stiff. Add sugar and beat well. Add coconut. Mix well and spread over cake mixture. Bake in a moderate oven for approximately 45 minutes.

Marble cake

120 g butter, softened
250 g caster sugar
3 eggs
1 cup self-raising flour
1 cup plain flour
¾ cup milk, at room temperature
1 teaspoon vanilla essence
1 rounded tablespoon cocoa
2 tablespoons hot water
Pink food colouring

Cream butter and sugar well, then add eggs one at a time, beating well after each addition. Fold in sifted flours alternately with the milk and vanilla. Divide mixture into three equal parts. Colour one part chocolate with the cocoa mixed with hot water and allowed to cool. Add pink colouring to second portion and leave third portion plain. Place alternate spoonfuls of mixture into a greased and lined deep 20 cm round or square tin. Shake down and run a knife through mixture to give a marbled effect. Bake in a moderate oven for about 1 hour or until a skewer inserted in the centre comes out clean. When cooked leave in tin for a few minutes before removing. Ice as desired.

This colourful cake is popular
for children's birthday parties.

Moist coconut cake

125 g butter, softened
1 cup caster sugar
½ teaspoon coconut essence
2 eggs
½ cup desiccated coconut
1½ cups self-raising flour, sifted
300 g sour cream
⅓ cup milk

COCONUT-ICE FROSTING
2 cups icing sugar
2 egg whites, lightly beaten
1⅓ cups desiccated coconut
Pink food colouring

Grease a 23 cm round cake tin, then line base with paper. Cream butter and sugar, add coconut essence, then beat in eggs one at a time, combining well. Stir in half the coconut and sifted flour with half the sour cream and milk, then stir in remaining ingredients. Bake in a moderate oven for about 1 hour. When cool, ice with coconut-ice frosting.

To make frosting, combine sifted icing sugar with egg whites, mix well, add coconut and a little colouring.

Orange and almond cake

2 navel oranges
6 eggs
250 g caster sugar
250 g ground almonds
1 teaspoon baking powder
Apricot jam for glaze or icing sugar, to decorate
Candied orange peel, to decorate

Place the oranges in a saucepan and boil gently for 2 hours until pulpy. Cool, then blend in a food processor until smooth. Beat eggs until very light and fluffy, then mix in sugar, almonds, baking powder and orange pulp. Pour mixture into a greased and lined 20–22 cm round cake tin and bake in a moderate oven for 1 hour. The cake should be very moist but firm. Cool for 10 minutes, then turn out onto a plate. Glaze with apricot jam, or dust with icing sugar and decorate with candied orange peel. Serve warm, with brandied oranges and cream.

Pineapple upside-down cake

1 cup caster sugar
1½ cups self-raising flour, sifted
2 eggs, lightly beaten
125 g butter, softened
⅔ cup milk
440 g tin pineapple circles, drained
Glacé cherries (optional)

Grease and line a deep 20 cm round cake tin. Place the sugar, flour, eggs, butter and milk into a bowl. Using an electric beater, mix at a medium speed for 4 minutes. Arrange pineapple circles on base of the tin and place a glacé cherry in the centre of each circle. Pour cake mixture over pineapple. Bake in a moderate oven for 60 minutes or until cooked when tested. Allow to stand for 10 minutes before turning out onto a plate.

Potato chocolate cake

60 g dark chocolate
125 g butter, softened
¾ cup caster sugar
⅔ cup mashed potato, cooled
⅓ cup cocoa
2 eggs
1½ cups self-raising flour
½ teaspoon salt
⅓ cup milk
Whipped cream, to fill

ICING
45 g dark chocolate
½ teaspoon oil
1 cup icing sugar, sifted

Melt chocolate. Cream butter, add sugar and potato and beat well. Add melted chocolate and sifted cocoa, then add eggs one at a time, beating well. Fold in sifted flour and salt alternately with milk. Spoon into two greased and lined 20 cm sandwich tins. Bake in a moderate oven for 25 minutes. Allow to cool then fill with whipped cream and top with icing.

ICING: To make icing, melt dark chocolate, oil and 2 tablespoons water in a bowl over simmering water. Gradually beat in icing sugar. Beat until smooth and spreadable. Quickly pour over cake and spread evenly.

Quick light fruit cake

470 g plain flour
1 teaspoon baking powder
250 g butter, softened
250 g caster sugar
4 large eggs
1 teaspoon vanilla
Pinch salt
375 g mixed dried fruit

Sift flour and baking powder. Combine all ingredients except mixed fruit in a large bowl and beat until creamy. Fold in mixed fruit. Spoon into a greased and lined deep 20 cm round tin. Bake in a low oven for 1¾ hours.

Pumpkin fruit cake

1 cup warm mashed pumpkin
125 g butter, softened
1 cup caster sugar
2 level tablespoons golden syrup
2 eggs
2 cups self-raising flour
Pinch salt
2¼ cups mixed dried fruit

Beat pumpkin, butter and sugar to a cream. Add the golden syrup and beat again. Add well-beaten eggs, flour, salt, and lastly, the fruit. Bake in a greased and lined deep 20 cm square cake tin in a moderately slow oven for 1–1½ hours or until cooked.

Rich mocha cake

275 g self-raising flour
50 g cocoa
5 g bicarbonate of soda
225 g caster sugar
5 g salt
125 g butter
1 tablespoon instant coffee powder or granules
75 ml hot water
175 ml milk
½ teaspoon vanilla essence
2 eggs

Sift flour, cocoa and bicarbonate of soda into a bowl. Mix in sugar and salt. Melt butter and fold into dry mixture. Dissolve coffee in hot water. Add milk, vanilla and coffee mixture to the flour mixture and fold in, beating until smooth. Add unbeaten eggs and beat for another few minutes. Pour into a well-greased and floured 24 cm ring tin and bake in a moderate oven for about 40 minutes, or until cooked when tested. Ice with chocolate or coffee icing.

Spiced apple cake

PASTRY
125 g butter
140 ml milk
2 cups self-raising flour, sifted
1 teaspoon salt

CREAM CHEESE FILLING
250 g cream cheese, softened
1/3 cup caster sugar
2 eggs
1 teaspoon vanilla

APPLE FILLING
4 large apples (about 850 g)
1/2 cup raisins
1/4 cup rum
1 teaspoon cinnamon
2 tablespoons sugar

To make pastry, melt butter in milk and allow to cool. Use a knife to mix in sifted flour and salt. Knead to form a soft dough. Set aside one-third of the pastry. Line a greased 20 cm springform cake tin with remaining pastry.

To make cream cheese filling, beat cream cheese until soft, add sugar, then beat until light and fluffy. Add eggs and vanilla; beat until smooth.

To make apple filling, peel and core apples and slice thinly. Mix with remaining apple filling ingredients.

Spread half the cream cheese mixture over base of pastry, spoon in apple filling, then pour over remaining cheese mixture. Press mixture down firmly. Crumble the remaining pastry over the top. Place the tin on a baking tray. Bake in a moderately slow oven for 1¾–2 hours until golden and cooked.

Sponge sandwich

4 eggs
¾ cup caster sugar
1 cup plain flour
1 teaspoon baking powder
Pinch salt
2 tablespoons milk
Vanilla
1 teaspoon butter

Separate eggs and beat whites until very stiff. Gradually add sugar, beating after each addition. Add yolks one at a time. Beat a little more. Lightly fold in flour, baking powder and salt which have been sifted together several times. Bring milk, vanilla, 2 tablespoons water and butter just to the boil, then stir in evenly. Pour into two 18 cm cake tins that have been well greased with butter and dusted with flour. Bake in a moderate oven for 25 minutes.

Pineapple coconut cake

2 cups self-raising flour
1 cup caster sugar
1 cup desiccated coconut
3 eggs, lightly beaten
450 g tin pineapple pieces in syrup, drained and chopped
150 g butter or margarine, melted

Grease a 22 cm round cake tin and line with baking paper.

Combine self-raising flour, caster sugar and coconut in a large bowl then add the eggs and the pineapple. Stir through the melted butter.

Pour into the tin and cook in a 180°C oven for 1¼ hours. Leave cake in tin for 5 minutes before turning out onto wire cake rack to cool.

Wholemeal date and honey cake

125 g butter
250 g pitted dates, chopped
2 tablespoons honey
⅔ cup milk
1 egg, lightly beaten
1 cup wholemeal self-raising flour
1 cup self-raising flour
½ cup raw sugar

Lightly grease a 20 cm ring tin and line with baking paper. Melt butter in a saucepan; add dates, honey, milk and egg. Stir mixture over a low heat for 1–2 minutes. Sift flours into a bowl, returning husks from sifter to mixture. Add sugar. Make a well in the centre of the dry ingredients, add date mixture and combine thoroughly. Spread mixture evenly into ring tin. Bake in a moderate oven for about 50 minutes. Leave cake in the tin for at least 5 minutes before turning it out onto a wire rack to cool.

Gluten-free muffins

1 cup brown rice flour
⅓ cup soy flour
2 teaspoons baking powder
½ teaspoon mixed spice
½ teaspoon cinnamon
1 cup rice bran
⅔ cup brown sugar (tightly packed)
1 cup mashed banana (2 medium bananas)
½ cup sultanas
½ cup chopped dried apricots
60 g dairy-free margarine, melted
1 cup soy milk

Preheat oven to 180°C. Grease a 12-hole standard muffin tin. Into a bowl sift together the rice flour, soy flour, baking powder, spice and cinnamon. Add the rice bran and brown sugar, then the mashed bananas, sultanas and apricots. Combine everything well. Lastly add the melted margarine and milk and mix until fully combined. Place mixture into prepared muffin tins and bake for 25 minutes.

These muffins are suitable for people with dairy, egg and gluten intolerances.

Peach blossom cake

125 g butter, softened
1 cup caster sugar
Whites of 4 eggs, at room temperature
1 cup plain flour
½ cup wheaten cornflour
1 teaspoon baking powder
½ cup milk, at room temperature
Pink food colouring

Preheat oven to 180°C. Grease and flour a 20 cm round tin. Cream butter and sugar until light and fluffy. Beat egg whites stiffly in another bowl and set aside. Sift the flours and baking powder together and add to the creamed mixture alternating with the milk, beginning and ending with flour. Gently fold the beaten egg whites through the mixture.

Divide the mixture into two portions and use the food colouring sparingly to tint one portion to a very pale pink. Put alternate spoonfuls of the two colours into the prepared tin. When all mixture is used, swirl the two colours together slightly by using the edge of a knife blade. Bake for 40–45 minutes or until cooked. Cool completely then ice the top of the cake with pale pink icing.

Lemon spiced coconut mini cupcakes

60 g butter, softened
¼ cup caster sugar
1 egg
¼ teaspoon vanilla essence
Grated zest of ½ lemon
¼ teaspoon mixed spice
Pinch salt
1 cup self-raising flour
½ cup coconut milk
rice bran oil, to grease

LEMON ICING
1 cup pure icing sugar, sifted
1 tablespoon lemon juice
1 drop pink food colouring
Pink sugar bows, for decoration

Using an electric beater and a medium-sized bowl, cream butter and caster sugar. Add egg, vanilla, zest, spice and salt, and beat well. Using a large spoon fold the sifted self-raising flour and coconut milk alternately into the creamed mixture until all ingredients are combined.

Grease two mini muffin tins with a small amount of rice bran oil, or place mini muffin papers in the tins. Fill each with a heaped teaspoon of mixture. Bake at 200°C for 15 minutes. Allow to cool before icing.

For the icing, combine all ingredients well. Ice cakes as desired, adding a pink sugar bow decoration on top (available from most supermarkets). Makes about 20.

Apple and cinnamon cake

90 g butter, softened
½ cup raw sugar
2 eggs
1½ cups wholemeal self-raising flour
1½ teaspoons cinnamon
175g low-fat natural yoghurt
½ cup low-fat milk
2 small green apples, cut into 2 cm cubes (about 2 cups)

COCONUT TOPPING
¼ cup loosely packed brown sugar
20 g butter, softened
1 tablespoon low-fat milk
½ cup moist flaked coconut or light desiccated coconut

Preheat oven to 180°C. Grease a 21 cm round springform tin. Line base and sides with baking paper. Place all cake ingredients except apple into a mixing bowl and beat using an electric mixer until combined. Stir through the apples. Pour mixture into tin. Bake for 40–45 minutes, until golden and cooked when tested with skewer.

Meanwhile, for the topping, combine all ingredients in a bowl. Remove cake from oven. Preheat oven grill to moderate. Spread topping evenly over warm cake in tin. Place tin under grill so topping is about 15 cm below element; grill 1–2 minutes until topping is melted and golden. Cool for 10 minutes before releasing spring. Cool completely.

Pears, plums or rhubarb can replace the apples.

Apple dessert cake (microwave)

60 g butter, softened
¾ cup caster sugar
1 teaspoon vanilla
1 egg
¾ cup milk
2 teaspoons baking powder
1½ cups plain flour
2 green cooking apples
1 teaspoon brown sugar
2 level teaspoons cinnamon
Cream or custard, to serve

Cream butter, sugar and vanilla. Beat in egg, then fold in milk. Add sifted baking powder and flour. Peel, core and thinly slice apples and place in bottom of a greased microwave-safe baking dish. Mix brown sugar and cinnamon into the batter mixture and pour over apples. Cook on high for 9–10 minutes. Let stand 5 minutes. Serve with cream or custard.

Quick mix cake

¼ cup milk
80 g soft butter or margarine
¾ cup caster sugar
2 eggs
1 cup self-raising flour
1 tablespoon cornflour
½ teaspoon vanilla (or to taste)
Pinch salt

Preheat oven to 180°C. Place all ingredients in bowl and beat well for 5 minutes at medium speed. Spoon into a greased and lined 20 x 10 cm loaf tin. Bake for 35 minutes or until a skewer comes out clean. Leave in the tin for a few minutes before turning out. When cold, ice as desired.

Sultana cake

500 g sultanas
¾ cup water (or use half sherry, half water)
250 g butter, softened
250 g caster sugar
1 dessertspoon cornflour
3 eggs (at room temperature)
315 g plain flour
1 teaspoon baking powder
Pinch salt

Place sultanas and water into a medium saucepan and boil over a medium heat until the sultanas have absorbed the liquid. Allow to cool completely.

Preheat oven to 150°C. Grease a 20 cm tin and line it with baking paper. Wrap several thicknesses of newspaper around the outside of prepared tin, securing well. Ensure the paper comes above the top of tin by about 5 cm.

Beat butter and sugar until light and fluffy and there are no visible signs of sugar granules. Dissolve the cornflour in ½ cup water and add to the butter mixture. Add the eggs one at a time, beating well after each. Fold in dry ingredients and lastly the sultanas. Place mixture in prepared tin, ensuring the mixture is pushed into the corners or edges. Smooth top. Bake for 2½–2¾ hours or until cooked when tested with a skewer.

When removing from oven, immediately wrap the entire cake (still in the tin) in a tea towel or thick bath towel and leave overnight to cool. Store in an airtight container.

Wholemeal boiled fruit cake

375 g mixed dried fruit
60 g dates, chopped
125 g butter
1 cup brown sugar
1 tablespoon golden syrup
1 egg
1 cup wholemeal plain flour
1 cup wholemeal self-raising flour
Pinch salt
⅓ cup chopped walnuts

Grease a deep 20 cm round cake tin and line with two pieces of baking paper, bringing paper 5 cm above edge of tin. Put mixed fruit, dates, butter, sugar, golden syrup and 1 cup water into a saucepan and stir over a low heat until the butter melts. Gradually bring to boil. Boil, uncovered, for 2 minutes. Remove from heat and cool completely.

Add lightly beaten egg to cooled fruit mixture and mix well. Add sifted dry ingredients and walnuts, then mix well. Spread evenly into prepared tin. Bake in a low oven for about 1¾ hours or until cooked. Remove and cover with foil. When cold, remove from tin and re-wrap in foil.

Potato fruit bun

60 g butter
½ cup caster sugar
½ cup cold mashed potato
1 egg
1 cup mixed dried fruit or sultanas
1 cup self-raising flour, sifted
¼ cup milk
½ teaspoon vanilla

Cream butter and sugar, then add mashed potato. Beat until well mixed. Add egg and fruit, then add sifted flour alternately with the milk and vanilla. Place in a greased and lined 20 x 10 x 7 cm loaf tin. Bake in moderate oven for 30–35 minutes.

Two-at-a-time cake

500 g self-raising flour
400 g caster sugar
5 eggs
1½ cups milk
1 teaspoon vanilla
250 g butter or margarine, softened

Sift flour and sugar together. Add eggs, milk, vanilla and butter. Beat together for 5 minutes. Pour into two greased and lined 20 cm round cake tins. Bake in a moderate oven for 30 minutes or until cooked when tested with a skewer.

Committee to build Ruth Fairfax House, c1950

Biscuits
and
slices

Cheese biscuits

120 g butter, softened
90 g cheddar cheese, grated
½ teaspoon salt
¼ teaspoon cayenne pepper
1 cup self-raising flour, sifted
1 cup crushed cornflakes (about 70 g)
1 egg
1 tablespoon milk

Cream butter until soft. Add cheese, salt, cayenne, sifted flour and cornflakes. Combine egg with milk. Reserve 2 teaspoons of this mixture for glazing. Add remaining egg mixture, mix and roll teaspoonfuls of mixture into balls. Place 5 cm apart on a greased tray, press with the back of a fork, then bake in a moderate oven for 8–10 minutes. Makes 24.

Burnt butter biscuits

125 g butter
125 g caster sugar
½ teaspoon vanilla
1 egg
185 g self-raising flour, sifted
Blanched almonds, to decorate

Place butter or margarine in a saucepan and heat until light brown in colour. Do not burn. Allow to cool. Cream melted butter and sugar. Add vanilla and egg, then flour, combining well. Roll small portions of mixture into balls and place a blanched almond in the centre of each. Place on a greased tray and bake in a moderate oven for 10–12 minutes.

Ginger creams

250 g butter, softened
250 g caster sugar
1 egg
1 tablespoon golden syrup
2½ cups plain flour
1 teaspoon bicarbonate of soda
Pinch salt
1 tablespoon ground ginger
Plain icing

Cream butter and sugar, add egg and golden syrup and beat. Sift in dry ingredients and mix well. Drop spoonfuls of the mixture onto a greased tray and bake in a moderate oven for 15–20 minutes. When cool, ice flat side of half of biscuits, then sandwich together with remaining biscuits.

Jam drops

125 g butter, softened
½ cup caster sugar
1 egg
1 teaspoon vanilla
½ teaspoon salt
1½ cups self-raising flour, sifted
Raspberry jam

Cream butter and sugar to a light consistency. Add egg, vanilla and salt then beat again until blended. Fold in sifted flour. Form into walnut-sized balls and place on a greased oven tray. Make an indentation in the centre and place a small quantity of jam in each. Bake in a moderately low oven for 15 minutes.

Irene's brown crunchies

140 g plain flour
1 teaspoon baking powder
125 g butter, softened
140 g caster sugar
1 egg
1 teaspoon vanilla
1 teaspoon honey
1 teaspoon bicarbonate of soda
1½ cups rolled oats
70 g desiccated coconut
Hot water

Sift flour with baking powder. Cream butter and sugar. Add egg, vanilla, honey, bicarbonate of soda, rolled oats and coconut to creamed mixture. Add flour, then sufficient hot water to make a dough (about 1 tablespoon). Roll into balls and place on a greased tray. Press balls with a fork to flatten slightly. Bake at 150°C for 30 minutes.

Orange biscuits

125 g butter, softened
½ cup caster sugar
1 egg, beaten
Grated zest of 1 orange
1 cup self-raising flour, sifted
1 cup desiccated coconut
1 cup rolled oats

Cream butter and sugar. Add egg, zest, flour, coconut and rolled oats, mixing well. Shape teaspoonfuls of mixture into rounds and place on a greased baking tray. Bake in a moderately hot oven for 10–12 minutes.

Shearers' cakes

4 cups self-raising flour
1 teaspoon cinnamon
1 teaspoon ground ginger
1 teaspoon mixed spice
1 cup caster sugar
1 cup sultanas
125 g butter, melted
2 tablespoons golden syrup
2 eggs, lightly beaten

Sift flour and spices into a bowl. Add sugar and sultanas. Combine melted butter, syrup and eggs. Add to dry ingredients. If too dry, add a little milk to make a kneading consistency. Knead well and press to a 1 cm thickness. Cut into rounds or shapes, place on a greased baking tray and bake in a moderate oven for 15 minutes or until cooked.

Shortbread

250 g butter, softened
¼ cup caster sugar
½ teaspoon vanilla
2 cups plain flour, sifted

Cream butter and sugar until light and fluffy. Mix in vanilla. Stir in sifted flour. Roll into balls, place on a greased tray and flatten with a fork. Bake in moderate oven for 12–15 minutes, or until pale golden.

Custard cream biscuits

BASE
185 g butter, softened
60 g icing sugar
60 g custard powder
1½ cups plain flour, sifted
½ teaspoon baking powder
Pinch salt

FILLING
2 tablespoons butter, softened
2 tablespoons sweetened condensed milk
2 tablespoons icing sugar

To make base, cream butter, icing sugar and custard powder, then add sifted flour, baking powder and salt. Roll into small balls and place on a greased baking tray. Flatten with a fork. Prick the top with a fork and cook in a moderately slow oven until a light brown.

To make filling, cream together ingredients and sandwich between biscuits.

Chocolate fudge squares

FUDGE SQUARES
250 g brown sugar
125 g butter
1 tablespoon cocoa
1 egg
1 teaspoon coffee essence
¼ teaspoon almond essence
½ teaspoon vanilla essence
1 tablespoon rum
250 g Scotch finger biscuits, crushed

CHOCOLATE ICING
90 g dark cooking chocolate
15 g butter, softened
1 cup icing sugar mixture, sifted
2 tablespoons hot water

For the fudge squares, combine all ingredients except biscuits in a saucepan and bring to the boil. Stir occasionally and simmer on low heat for 3 minutes. Add the crushed biscuits and stir through. Pour into a greased and lined 18 cm x 28 cm baking tin.

For the icing, melt the chocolate over hot water in a double saucepan. Add the butter, icing mixture and hot water. Stir until smooth then spread over slice. Refrigerate until set. Cut into squares. Serve with tea or coffee.

Anzac biscuits

1 cup plain (all-purpose) flour
⅔ cup caster sugar
1 cup rolled oats
1 cup desiccated coconut
125 g unsalted butter
¼ cup golden syrup
½ teaspoon bicarbonate of soda
1 tablespoon boiling water

Sift flour and sugar into a bowl. Add oats and coconut; make a well in the centre. Combine butter and golden syrup in a small saucepan. Stir over low heat until butter has melted and mixture is smooth; remove from heat. Dissolve bicarbonate of soda in boiling water; add immediately to butter mixture. Add butter mixture to dry ingredients. Using a wooden spoon, stir until well combined.

Drop one level tablespoon of mixture at a time onto a greased and lined 32 x 28 cm biscuit tray. Flatten gently, allowing room for spreading. Bake in a moderate oven for 20 minutes or until just browned. Remove from oven and transfer to a wire rack to cool.

Orange walnut shortbread

185 g butter, chilled and cubed
¼ cup caster sugar
2 teaspoons finely grated orange zest (see Variation)
1¼ cups plain flour
2 tablespoons rice flour
¼ cup finely chopped walnuts
Icing sugar, for dusting

Place butter, sugar, zest and flours in a large mixing bowl. Using fingertips, rub the mixture together until it forms a soft dough. Press the dough together lightly until smooth. Roll the mixture out between two sheets of baking paper to a thickness of about 1 cm.

Using a 4 cm round cutter, cut shapes from dough. Sprinkle chopped walnuts over the biscuits, pressing lightly to make them stick. Transfer to a greased and lined tray and bake in a moderate oven for 15–20 minutes, until golden. Dust with icing sugar while still warm.

Shortbread can be stored for up to 3 days in an airtight container.

VARIATION: Use lemon zest instead of orange, if desired, or a combination of the two.

To store these biscuits, lay sheets of baking paper between layers of biscuits to protect their coating.

Apple slice

BASE
125 g butter, softened
½ cup caster sugar
1 egg
1½ cups self-raising flour, sifted

FILLING
4 medium apples
2 teaspoons lemon juice
½ cup caster sugar
¼ teaspoon ground cloves
½ teaspoon cinnamon
Passionfruit icing

To make base, cream butter and sugar, then add egg. Fold in sifted flour. Press half of the mixture into a small slice tin. Roll out the second half, ready to cover filling.

To make filling, peel and core apples, slice and cook in ½ cup water and lemon juice until tender. Drain and mash roughly, then add sugar, cloves and cinnamon. While mixture is still hot, spoon over base. Cover with the second layer of pastry and bake in a moderate oven for 25 minutes or until cooked. When cool, top with passionfruit icing.

*One or more of the apples can be
replaced with chokos.*

Apricot ginger fingers

90 g dried apricots
1½ cups self-raising flour
1½ tablespoons cocoa
Pinch salt
¼ teaspoon cinnamon
125 g butter, chilled and cubed
¾ cup caster sugar
60 g chopped pecan nuts
90 g chopped crystallised ginger
1 egg, beaten
1 cup milk
Lemon icing (see page 142)

Soak apricots in just enough boiling water to cover the fruit. Leave for 30 minutes, until soft but not pulpy. Drain off excess liquid (see Note).

Sift flour, cocoa, salt and cinnamon. Rub in butter, then add sugar, nuts, ginger and chopped apricots. Mix well. Fold in egg and milk. Spread into a greased and lined 25 x 30 cm Swiss roll tin. Bake in a moderate oven for 25–30 minutes. Allow to cool, then top with lemon icing. Cut into finger lengths when icing is set.

NOTE: Strained juice from apricots may be used instead of milk.

Fruit and walnut slice

1 cup sultanas
1 cup currants
2 cups caster sugar
125 g butter
4 cups plain flour, sifted
1 teaspoon bicarbonate of soda
1 teaspoon each of cinnamon, ginger, mixed spice and nutmeg
½ cup chopped walnuts

Boil the sultanas, currants, sugar, butter and 2 cups water together for 5 minutes, then allow to cool. Add sifted flour, bicarbonate of soda and spices. Stir in the walnuts. Spread mixture evenly into a 20 cm round tin or a 19 x 29 cm rectangular slice tin that has been greased and lined with two layers of baking paper. Bake in a slow oven for 1½ hours.

Coconut delight

1 cup self-raising flour
1 tablespoon cocoa
1 cup cornflakes
½ cup caster sugar
1 cup desiccated coconut, plus extra for decoration
⅔ cup butter
1 dessertspoon golden syrup
½ teaspoon vanilla
Chocolate icing
Desiccated coconut, for sprinkling

Sift flour and cocoa. Add cornflakes, sugar and coconut. Melt butter, golden syrup and vanilla and mix into dry ingredients. Press into a greased and lined 17 x 26 cm tray and bake in a moderate oven for 20–25 minutes. When cold, top with chocolate icing and sprinkle with coconut.

Caramel slice

BASE
1 cup self-raising flour, sifted
1 cup brown sugar
1 cup desiccated coconut
125 g butter, melted

FILLING
400 g tin sweetened condensed milk
60 g butter
2 tablespoons golden syrup
½ teaspoon gelatine
2 tablespoons boiling water

TOPPING
60 g butter
1 tablespoon golden syrup
1 cup desiccated coconut
½ cup rolled oats

To make base, combine flour, sugar, coconut and butter, mix well and press into a greased and lined 18 x 28 cm slice tin. Bake in a moderate oven for 20–25 minutes or until light golden. Cool slightly.

To make filling, heat condensed milk, butter and golden syrup in a saucepan until all ingredients are melted, stirring to combine. Stir through gelatine dissolved in boiling water. Stir continuously over medium heat for 10–15 minutes until caramel-brown. Cool slightly. Spread filling over base.

To make topping, melt together butter and golden syrup, then stir in coconut and oats. Mix well. Sprinkle over filling. Bake in a moderate oven for 15–20 minutes, until golden brown. Cool in tin, then cut into small squares. Not suitable for freezing.

Cherry and walnut slice

BASE
2 large tablespoons butter, softened
¼ cup brown sugar
1 heaped cup self-raising flour, sifted

TOPPING
2 eggs
1¼ cups brown sugar
4 tablespoons flour
1 teaspoon baking powder
½ cup drained pitted black cherries
½ cup walnuts
1 cup desiccated coconut

To make base, combine butter, sugar and flour and press into a greased and lined 18 x 26 cm slice tin. Bake in a moderate oven for 8 minutes.

To make topping, beat eggs and sugar. Add remaining ingredients. Spread over partly cooked base and return to oven for 20–25 minutes or until firm and golden. Mark into squares while still warm.

Chocolate peppermint slice

BASE
125 g butter
2 tablespoons cocoa
2 eggs, beaten
1 cup caster sugar
1 cup plain flour, sifted
½ teaspoon baking powder
Pinch salt
¾ cup sultanas
1 teaspoon vanilla

TOPPING
2 tablespoons butter
1 cup icing sugar, sifted
1 tablespoon cream
½ teaspoon peppermint essence
125 g dark chocolate, melted

To make base, gently melt butter with cocoa, stirring to combine. Beat the eggs and sugar, and fold in cooled cocoa mixture. Combine with sifted flour, baking powder and salt, then add sultanas and vanilla. Pour mixture into a greased and lined 18 x 30 cm slice tin. Bake in a moderate oven for 20–25 minutes. Allow to cool.

To make topping, beat butter, icing sugar and cream together, then add peppermint essence. Spread over base, then top with chocolate.

VARIATION: Add 1 cup chopped walnuts to the base and, for the topping, omit peppermint and add 1 teaspoon vanilla.

Chocolate rough slice

BASE
140 g self-raising flour
Pinch salt
2 teaspoons cocoa
125 g caster sugar
40 g desiccated coconut
125 g butter, melted

TOPPING
½ cup sweetened condensed milk
1 cup icing sugar, sifted
1 cup desiccated coconut
1 tablespoon cocoa
1 teaspoon vanilla
35 g butter, melted

To make base, sift flour, salt and cocoa together, add sugar and coconut, then stir in butter. Mix well and press into an 18 x 26 cm slice tin. Bake in a moderate oven for 25 minutes.

To make topping, combine all ingredients over medium heat, stirring, until well mixed. Pour over base while still warm. Smooth top with a spatula dipped in hot water. Allow topping to set, then cut into slices.

Chocolate caramel shortbread

BASE
125 g butter or margarine
½ cup caster sugar
1 cup plain flour, sifted

CARAMEL
400 g tin sweetened condensed milk
½ cup sugar
3 tablespoons golden syrup
125 g butter or margarine
½ teaspoon gelatine
2 tablespoons boiling water

ICING
90 g dark chocolate
30 g butter or margarine

To make base, cream butter and sugar until light and fluffy, then stir in sifted flour in two lots. When mixture becomes too difficult to stir, use hands to press ingredients together. Knead lightly until smooth. Press evenly over base of a greased and lined 18 x 28 cm lamington tin, then bake in a moderate oven for 20 minutes, or until golden brown. Leave to cool in tin.

To make caramel, combine all ingredients (except gelatine and boiling water) in a saucepan with a heavy base. Stir over low heat until butter melts and sugar dissolves. Continue stirring, gradually bringing mixture to the boil. Stir through gelatine dissolved in boiling water. Reduce heat and simmer, stirring constantly, for about 5 minutes or until golden brown. Pour hot mixture over completely cooled base and allow to cool.

To make icing, melt chocolate in a heatproof dish over a pan of simmering water, add butter, then stir until melted. Spread evenly over the cooled caramel mixture. When cooled, cut into squares.

Coffee slice

BASE
125 g butter, softened
55 g caster sugar
150 g plain flour, sifted
40 g self-raising flour, sifted

FILLING
400 g tin sweetened condensed milk
30 g butter
2 tablespoons golden syrup
3 teaspoons instant coffee powder
40 g finely chopped walnuts

TOPPING
150 g plain flour
2 teaspoons cinnamon
55 g brown sugar (firmly packed)
125 g butter

For the base, cream butter and sugar until just combined, then stir in flours. Mix to a firm dough. Press evenly over the base of a well-greased 25 x 30 cm Swiss roll tin. Bake in a moderate oven for 10 minutes, then spread with filling while still hot.

For the filling, combine condensed milk, butter, golden syrup and coffee in a saucepan, then stir over medium heat until mixture begins to bubble. Continue stirring briskly for about 3 minutes, or until mixture is thick. Stir in walnuts. Spread over the hot base.

To make topping, sift dry ingredients into a large bowl, then rub in butter. Mix to a firm dough, gather into a ball, wrap in plastic wrap and refrigerate for 30 minutes. Grate topping evenly over surface of filling and bake for a further 10–15 minutes, until firm to the touch. Cool in pan then cut into slices.

Easy fruit slice

250 g butter
1 cup brown sugar
1 cup mixed dried fruit
¼ cup chopped nuts or 1 cup fruit medley
1 egg
½ teaspoon vanilla
1½ cups self-raising flour
Pinch salt

Melt butter in saucepan, add sugar, stir and remove from heat. Add fruit and nuts, beat in egg and vanilla, then fold in flour and salt. Spread mixture in a greased and lined lamington tin and bake in a moderate oven for 20–25 minutes. When cool, cut into finger lengths.

Lattice cream slice

250 g cream cheese, softened
250 g unsalted butter, softened
1 cup caster sugar
1 dessertspoon gelatine
¼ cup boiling water
2 packets Lattice biscuits
Icing sugar

Cream together the cheese, butter and sugar. Dissolve gelatine in boiling water, add to cheese mixture and mix well. Line a Swiss roll tin with foil. Place biscuits from 1 packet on the foil, dull side facing up. Spread creamed mixture over biscuits and top with remaining packet of biscuits, shiny side up. Sift icing sugar over top to decorate. Chill until ready to serve.

Ginger fantasy bar

BASE
250 g butter, softened
125 g caster sugar
2 cups self-raising flour, sifted
1 teaspoon ground ginger

TOPPING
2 eggs
1¼ cups brown sugar
¾ cup raisins
¼ cup chopped nuts
¼ cup chopped glacé cherries
¼ cup chopped glacé ginger
1 cup desiccated coconut
90 g self-raising flour

To make the base, cream butter and sugar, then add sifted flour and ginger. Press into a greased and lined 20 x 30 cm slice tin. Bake in a moderate oven until partly cooked (about 15 minutes).

To make topping, beat eggs and sugar together until fluffy. Add remaining ingredients and pour over the hot half-cooked base. Return to oven and bake a further 30–35 minutes, or until a skewer comes out clean. If surface is browning too quickly, cover tin with baking paper or foil.

Lemon fruit slice

125 g butter
1 dessertspoon golden syrup
1 teaspoon vanilla
1 cup self-raising flour, sifted
½ cup caster sugar
1 cup desiccated coconut
1 cup chopped mixed dried fruit
Pinch salt
Lemon icing (p142)

Melt butter, then add the golden syrup and vanilla. Combine remaining ingredients, then add the butter mixture and mix well. Press into a greased and lined 20 x 30 cm lamington tin and bake in a moderate oven for about 20 minutes. Ice with lemon icing while still hot. Cut into squares when cold.

Rhubarb slice

300 g rhubarb, trimmed and cut into 5 mm slices
1½ cups caster sugar, plus 1 tablespoon extra for sprinkling
185 g butter, softened
½ teaspoon vanilla essence
3 eggs
¾ cup plain flour
¾ teaspoon baking powder

Combine rhubarb and ½ cup sugar and let stand for 1 hour, stirring occasionally. Strain, discarding liquid. Cream butter, remaining 1 cup sugar and vanilla, then add eggs one at a time, beating well after each addition. Sift flour and baking powder over mixture, then stir to combine. Spread mixture evenly over the base of a greased and lined 20 x 30 cm slice tin. Put rhubarb over top in a single layer. Sprinkle with extra sugar and bake in a moderate oven for 40–45 minutes or until golden. Cool slightly in tin then lift out and cut into squares. Best eaten on day it is made.

No-bake chocolate slice

125 g butter
125 g caster sugar
1 dessertspoon drinking chocolate
1 packet plain biscuits, crushed
1 egg
200 g fruit and nut chocolate
60 g Copha

Melt butter with the sugar, add drinking chocolate and biscuits and bring
to the boil. Cool and add well-beaten egg. Press into a slice pan and place
in refrigerator. Melt chocolate and Copha, then pour over the firm base.
Refrigerate until set.

Old-fashioned raisin bars

1 cup chopped raisins
125 g butter
1 cup caster sugar
1 egg, beaten
1¾ cups plain flour
1 level teaspoon bicarbonate of soda
1 teaspoon each nutmeg, ground cloves and allspice
Pinch salt
½ cup chopped walnuts
Icing sugar, sifted, for sprinkling

Place raisins in saucepan, add 1 cup water and bring to the boil. Remove
from heat and add butter. Cool until lukewarm, then stir in sugar and egg.
Sift together dry ingredients and add to the mixture. Stir in walnuts. Pour
into a greased and lined 20 x 30 cm baking tin and bake in a moderate
oven for approximately 20 minutes. Remove from pan and cut into bars.
Sprinkle with icing sugar.

Opera house slice

BASE
125 g butter, melted
½ cup icing sugar
1 cup plain flour, sifted

TOPPING
60 g butter
⅓ cup caster sugar
1 tablespoon milk
1 teaspoon vanilla
1½ cups mixed dried fruit
¼ cup slivered almonds

To make base, mix butter, icing sugar and sifted flour together, then press into a greased and lined 17 x 27 cm slice tin. Cook in a 180°C oven for 10–12 minutes until brown and cooked through.

To make topping, melt butter, then add sugar, milk, vanilla and mixed dried fruit. Heat until bubbling, then add almonds. Spread over base, then return to oven and cook for 5–10 minutes until bubbling. Cool in tin then slice into squares or fingers.

Passionfruit shortbread

BASE
125 g butter
1¾ cups self-raising flour, sifted
½ cup caster sugar, plus extra for sprinkling
1 egg, beaten
½ teaspoon vanilla
Pinch salt

FILLING
1 tablespoon butter, softened
1 cup icing sugar, sifted
Pulp of 2 passionfruit

To make base, rub butter into flour until it resembles breadcrumbs, then add sugar. Add egg, vanilla and salt, mixing to form a dry, crumbly mixture. Press into a greased and lined 18 cm round tin, rough up the surface with a fork and sprinkle with extra sugar. Bake in a moderate oven for about 40 minutes. When cold, slice through the middle and fill.

To make filling, cream together butter, icing sugar and passionfruit pulp.

*Passionfruit shortbread keeps very well
and is ideal for freezing.*

Passionfruit slice

BASE
125 g butter or margarine, softened
½ cup caster sugar
1 egg
1½ cups self-raising flour, sifted

TOPPING
400 g tin sweetened condensed milk
225 g tin reduced cream
½ cup lemon juice (2 lemons)
3 rounded tablespoons custard powder (90 g)
1 cup caster sugar
3 passionfruit

To make base, cream butter and sugar, add well-beaten egg, fold in sifted flour and press mixture into a greased and lined 20 x 30 cm lamington tin. Bake at 180°C for 15 minutes or until golden brown. Allow to cool.

To make topping, combine sweetened condensed milk, reduced cream and lemon juice. Spread over base. Blend custard powder, sugar and 2 cups water and boil for 5 minutes or until thickened, stirring constantly. Add passionfruit pulp, pour over filling and chill.

Date and ginger slice

Melted butter or oil, for brushing
1 cup self-raising flour, sifted
½ cup caster sugar
1 teaspoon ground ginger
1 cup desiccated coconut
1 cup chopped dates
½ cup chopped walnuts
2 teaspoons grated lime zest
180 g butter, melted
1 egg, lightly beaten

ICING
1 cup icing sugar
15 g butter, melted, extra
3 teaspoons lime juice

Preheat oven to 180°C. Brush a 27 x 18 cm rectangular cake tin with melted butter or oil. Cover base with non-stick paper, extending over two sides. Place flour, sugar, ginger, coconut, dates, walnuts and zest into medium-sized mixing bowl. Using a wooden spoon, stir until well combined. Add melted butter and mix well. Add egg and mix well. Press mixture into prepared tin. Bake for 20–25 minutes, or until lightly golden. Stand for 5 minutes before lifting out onto rack to cool.

For the icing, combine icing sugar, extra 15 g butter and lime juice. Spread evenly over slice and let stand until set.

Nita's date slice

2 cups self-raising flour, sifted
1 cup brown sugar
145 g butter, chilled and cubed
1 egg
1 cup milk
1 teaspoon baking powder
1 cup chopped dates

ICING
1½ cups icing sugar
10 g butter, softened
2 tablespoons milk
¼ teaspoon coffee essence

Preheat oven to 180°C. Grease and flour a 17 x 27 cm slice tin. Place the flour and brown sugar in mixing bowl. Rub in butter with fingertips until well combined and crumbly. Place half of this dry mixture into a greased and lined slice tin, pressing down firmly.

Mix together egg, milk and baking powder. Add chopped dates, stir to combine and add all of this mixture into second half of mixture in bowl. Pour over base mixture in tin. Bake in preheated oven for 30–40 minutes.

For the icing, combine all ingredients until smooth. When the slice is cold, ice and cut into 24 pieces.

NOTE: The slice freezes well, but is more presentable if you ice it after thawing. You can also substitute any dried fruit for the dates.

Honeycomb cheesecake slice

BASE
¾ cup self-raising flour
⅓ cup brown sugar
⅓ cup desiccated coconut
1 tablespoon cocoa
90 g butter, melted

TOPPING
500 g cream cheese
⅓ cup caster sugar
½ cup sour cream
2 teaspoons gelatine
1½ tablespoons hot water
100g chocolate coated honeycomb bars or pieces

Preheat the oven to 180°C. Spray a 30 x 20 cm slice tin with non-stick cooking spray. For the base, mix ingredients until combined. Press mixture into the prepared tin and bake for 15–20 minutes. Remove from oven and allow to cool.

In a bowl, beat the cream cheese, sugar and sour cream together until smooth. Dissove gelatine in hot water and beat into the cheese mixture. Roughly chop the honeycomb and fold into the mixture. Pour over the cooled base and leave to set in refrigerator.

Lemon slice

SHORTBREAD BASE
125 g butter or margarine, softened
125 g caster sugar
1 egg
250 g plain flour

LEMON FILLING
1 cup sugar
Grated zest and juice of 3 lemons
½ cup cornflour, blended with ⅓ cup cold water

CREAM TOPPING
1½ cups milk
1½ tablespoons caster sugar
1½ tablespoons cornflour
1 teaspoon butter
1 teaspoon vanilla
¼ cup desiccated coconut

For the base, cream butter and sugar, add egg and mix well. Add flour and mix to a stiff dough. Press into base of lightly greased shallow tin. Bake in a moderate oven for 20–25 minutes.

For filling, place sugar, lemon juice, zest and 1¼ cups water in a saucepan. Bring to the boil. Thicken with blended cornflour. Cook for 1 minute, stirring constantly. Cool slightly. Pour over base and chill until firm.

For the cream topping, heat milk and sugar together, stir in cornflour blended with 3 tablespoons of water. Cook until thickened, stirring constantly. Add butter and vanilla. Stir until butter has melted. Pour over lemon layer. Sprinkle with coconut. Allow to cool then cut into squares.

Marshmallow bars

BASE
125 g butter
2½ tablespoons cocoa
½ cup caster sugar
1 egg, beaten
1¼ teaspoons vanilla
¾ cup sultanas
1 cup desiccated coconut
1½ cups wheatmeal biscuit crumbs

TOPPING
4½ tablespoons gelatine
4 cups caster sugar
1 teaspoon vanilla
1 tablespoon lemon juice
Pink food colouring (optional)

For the base, melt butter, cocoa and sugar and boil until sugar is dissolved. Remove from heat, cool then add egg and vanilla. Stir in sultanas, coconut and biscuit crumbs and mix well. Press into a greased and lined 20 x 30 cm lamington tray. Chill in refrigerator.

For topping, add gelatine to 1 cup cold water and stand for 5 minutes. Combine sugar and 1½ cups water in a large saucepan and stir constantly over medium heat until sugar is dissolved. Add the gelatine and boil for 20 minutes longer. Allow to cool then add vanilla, lemon juice and colouring, if using, and beat until stiff. Pour over base and chill until set. Cut slice into bars.

Prune bars

125 g butter, softened
¾ cup caster sugar
3 eggs
1½ cups plain flour
1½ teaspoons baking powder
2 heaped tablespoons cocoa
¼ cup milk
½ cup chopped walnuts
1 cup chopped pitted prunes
Chocolate icing

Cream butter and sugar. Add eggs one at a time. Sift flour, baking powder and cocoa together and mix with milk, then add nuts and prunes. Bake in a greased and lined 20 x 30 cm tin in a moderate oven for 20–25 minutes. While warm, ice with chocolate icing.

Chocolate marshmallow slice

200 g marshmallows
60 g butter
125 g dark chocolate, chopped
1 teaspoon vanilla
125 g walnuts, chopped
Brandy or rum, optional

Place marshmallows, butter and 1 tablespoon water in the microwave for 2 minutes on medium high. Remove, then stir in chocolate and vanilla until chocolate has melted. Beat until smooth and creamy, then add nuts and brandy or rum, if using. Spread in a greased and lined bar tin and refrigerate overnight. Cut into small squares.

Cashew brownies

200 g chopped dark chocolate
175 g butter, chopped
2 eggs
1 cup soft brown sugar
1 cup plain flour
⅓ cup cocoa
½ cup unsalted cashews, toasted and chopped
100 g chopped dark chocolate, extra

ICING
200 g chopped dark chocolate
½ cup sour cream
¼ cup icing sugar

Preheat oven to 160°C. Lightly grease a 23 cm square shallow tin and line base with baking paper.

Melt chocolate and butter in a heatproof bowl over (not touching) simmering water, stirring to combine. Allow to cool.

Whisk eggs and sugar in a large bowl for 5 minutes, or until pale and thick. Fold in cooled chocolate mixture, then sifted flour and cocoa. Fold in cashews and extra chocolate, then pour into tin, smoothing the top. Bake for 30–35 minutes, or until just firm to the touch; do not overcook. (The brownies may have a slightly soft centre when hot but will firm when cool.) Allow to cool.

For the icing, melt chocolate in a small heatproof bowl over (not touching) simmering water, stirring frequently. Allow to cool slightly, then add sour cream and icing sugar and mix well. Spread evenly over cooled brownies. Leave for a few hours or overnight to firm, then cut into squares.

Store in an airtight container for up to 5 days, or freeze for up to 3 months.

Muesli slice

250 g butter, diced
2 tablespoons honey
1 cup caster sugar
2½ cups rolled oats
¾ cup desiccated coconut
1 cup cornflakes, lightly crushed
½ cup flaked almonds
1 teaspoon ground mixed spice
45 g finely chopped dried apricots
1 cup dried mixed fruit

Preheat oven to 160°C. Grease a 20 x 30 cm tin and line with baking paper, leaving paper hanging over two long sides.

Combine butter, honey and sugar in a small saucepan and stir over low heat for 5 minutes, or until butter has melted and sugar has dissolved.

Mix remaining ingredients together in a bowl and make a well in the centre. Pour in butter mixture and stir well, then press into the tin. Bake for 45 minutes or until golden. Cool completely in the tin, then refrigerate for 2 hours or until firm.

Lift slice from tin using paper as handles. Cut into pieces. Store in an airtight container for up to 3 days. Makes 18.

Newcastle Seaside Home, c1931

Breads

Damper

3 cups self-raising flour, plus extra for sifting
3 teaspoons salt
90 g butter, chilled and cubed
1 cup water
1 cup milk, plus extra for brushing

Sift flour and salt into a bowl, then rub in butter until mixture resembles fine breadcrumbs. Make a well in the centre, add combined water and milk, then mix lightly with a sharp knife, using a cutting motion.

Turn out onto a lightly floured board. Form lightly into a round and place on a greased oven tray. With a sharp knife, make a cross about 1 cm deep across the dough. Brush top of dough with milk and sift a little extra flour over it. Bake in a hot oven for about 10 minutes or until golden brown, then reduce heat to moderate and cook for a further 15 minutes.

Jungle scones

2 cups self-raising flour
1 teaspoon baking powder
30 g butter
1 egg
⅔ cup cold milk
⅓ cup hot water
½ teaspoon salt
1½ tablespoons grated cheese
1 tablespoon grated parmesan
½ cup chopped parsley
¼ cup chopped chives
¼ cup other green herbs (such as mint, basil, rosemary)
Pinch mustard powder
Grated cheese, extra (optional)

Sift flour and baking powder. Rub in butter with fingertips until mixture is fine and crumbly. Reserve ½ cup of this mixture. Beat egg, milk, water and salt together. Add all other ingredients. Combine with 1½ cups flour mixture, stir vigorously, then add reserved ½ cup flour mixture. There is no need to roll out scones; simply drop soupspoon-sized pieces onto a cold greased baking tray. Sprinkle with a little grated cheese. Bake in a hot oven for 10–12 minutes. Makes 12–14 scones.

Plain scones

¾ cup cream
1 cup milk
3 rounded tablespoons icing sugar, sifted
3 cups self-raising flour, sifted

With a rotary beater, beat together cream, milk and icing sugar for 1 minute. Add sifted flour and combine. Press onto a flat surface and cut into desired shapes. Place on a greased and floured baking tray and cook in a hot oven for 12–15 minutes.

Potato scones

1½ cups self-raising flour
1 cup cold mashed potato
30 g butter
¾–1 cup milk, plus extra
½ cup coarsely grated tasty cheese

Sift flour into a bowl, add mashed potato and stir to combine. Add butter and milk and mix to form a soft dough. Turn onto a lightly floured surface. Knead dough lightly. Divide into eight portions. Roll each into a thin sausage, about 25 cm long. Shape the rolls into knots and place on a baking tray that has been dusted with flour.

Brush tops of knots with extra milk and sprinkle with grated cheese. Bake in a hot oven for 15–20 minutes or until scones are golden and cooked through. Serve scones warm, spread with butter.

*Potato scones are delicious served
with a hearty casserole.*

Sultana scone slice

2½ cups self-raising flour
¼ cup icing sugar
1 teaspoon cinnamon, plus extra for sprinkling
Pinch salt
60 g butter, chilled and cubed
½ cup sultanas
1 egg, lightly beaten
¾ cup milk
Coffee sugar crystals

Sift flour, icing sugar, cinnamon and salt into a bowl. Rub butter into mixture. Add sultanas. Combine beaten egg and milk, then mix into dry ingredients. Press into a small well-greased slice tin or 18 cm square cake tin. Sprinkle top with coffee sugar crystals and extra cinnamon, if desired. Bake in a hot oven for 15 minutes. Allow to cool before cutting.

VARIATION: Add 1 teaspoon ginger and 1 teaspoon mixed spice.

Pumpkin scones

1 tablespoon butter
1 cup caster sugar
1 cup mashed pumpkin
1 egg
3 cups self-raising flour

Beat butter and sugar to a cream, then add the mashed pumpkin and egg. Stir in flour. If too stiff, add a little milk. Turn onto a board, roll out and cut into desired shapes. Place on a greased tray and bake in a hot oven for 15–20 minutes.

Cheese scones

250 g self-raising flour
1 teaspoon baking powder
½ teaspoon dry mustard
Pinch salt
30 g butter, chilled and cubed
25 g grated parmesan
90 g finely grated cheddar cheese
1 cup milk

Preheat oven to 220°C. Lightly grease a baking tray or line it with baking paper. Sift flour, baking powder, mustard and salt into a bowl. Using fingertips, rub in butter until mixture resembles fine breadcrumbs. Stir in parmesan and 60 g of the cheddar cheese, making sure they don't clump together. Make a well in the centre.

Add almost all the milk and cut in with a flat-bladed knife until dough comes together in clumps. Add some of the remaining milk if necessary. With floured hands, gently gather dough together, lift out onto a lightly floured surface and pat into a ball. Do not knead or scones will be tough.

Pat the dough out to a 2 cm thickness. Cut into 5 cm rounds. Gather the trimmings and, without over-handling, press out as before and cut more rounds. Place rounds close together on the prepared tray and sprinkle with the remaining cheese. Bake for 12–15 minutes, or until risen and golden. Serve warm.

White loaf

2½ teaspoons instant dried yeast
1 teaspoon caster sugar
300 ml warm water
450 g white bread flour
2 teaspoons salt

Sprinkle yeast and sugar over 150 ml warm water in a small bowl. Stir to dissolve sugar, then leave in a draught-free place for 10 minutes, or until yeast is foamy.

Combine flour and salt in bowl of an electric mixer with a dough hook attachment and make a well in the centre. Add remaining warm water to yeast mixture, then pour this mixture into the well. Mix on lowest speed for 2 minutes or until a dough forms. Increase speed to medium and knead dough for another 10 minutes, or until it is smooth and elastic.

Alternatively, mix by hand with a wooden spoon, then turn onto a floured work surface and knead dough for 10 minutes or until smooth and elastic.

Grease a large bowl with oil then transfer dough to the bowl, turning dough to coat it in oil. Cover with plastic wrap and leave to rise in a draught-free place for 1–1½ hours or until dough has doubled in size.

Knock back dough by punching it gently, then turn out onto a lightly floured surface. Shape into a round and transfer to a greased baking tray. Cover loosely with a damp cloth and leave for 30 minutes, or until doubled in size. Meanwhile, preheat oven to 190ºC.

Using a sharp knife, make three diagonal slashes about 4 cm apart on top of loaf. Bake for 40 minutes, or until loaf sounds hollow when tapped on the base. Transfer to a wire rack to cool completely.

Wholemeal bread

1 teaspoon soft brown sugar
15 g fresh (compressed) yeast or 7 g sachet dried yeast
1¼ cups warm water or milk
3¼ cups wholemeal plain flour
1 teaspoon salt
Milk, extra, for brushing

Brush a deep loaf tin with oil or melted butter. Combine sugar and yeast in a medium bowl. Gradually add water or milk; blend until smooth. Cover with plastic wrap and stand in a warm place for about 10 minutes or until yeast is foamy.

Sift flour and salt into large mixing bowl. Make a well in the centre. Add yeast mixture and use a flat-bladed knife to mix to a soft dough.

Turn onto a lightly floured surface and knead for 5–10 minutes or until smooth. Shape the dough into a ball and place in a large, lightly oiled mixing bowl. Cover with plastic wrap and leave in a warm, draught-free place for 15–20 minutes or until well risen. Knock back dough by punching it down lightly. Knead again for 3–5 minutes or until smooth. Place dough in prepared tin. Cover with plastic wrap and leave in a warm, draught-free place until well risen and dough has doubled in size.

Meanwhile, preheat oven to moderately hot. Brush loaf with a little milk. Make slits or patterns in the top with a sharp knife and/or sprinkle with a little extra flour if desired. Bake for 35–40 minutes or until well browned and cooked through. Stand bread in tin for 5 minutes before transferring to wire rack to cool.

Banana health bread

1 cup All-Bran
1 cup milk
1 cup wholemeal self-raising flour, sifted
1 teaspoon bicarbonate of soda
½ cup raw sugar
½ cup sultanas
½ cup chopped dried apricots
1 cup desiccated coconut
½ cup wheatgerm
3 bananas
2 eggs

Place All-Bran in a small bowl, cover with milk and allow to stand for 10–15 minutes. Combine sifted flour and soda, sugar, sultanas, apricots, coconut and wheatgerm. Stir well.

In another bowl, mash bananas thoroughly, add eggs, then stir to combine. Add banana mixture and soaked bran to dry ingredients. Mix well. Spoon mixture into a greased loaf tin and bake in a moderately slow to moderate oven for approximately 1 hour or until cooked when tested with a skewer.

*This bread is particularly delicious
toasted and buttered.*

Beer bread rolls

2⅔ cups plain (all-purpose) flour, plus extra if needed
3 teaspoons baking powder
1 tablespoon sugar
50 g butter, chopped
1 teaspoon salt
375 ml beer

Process flour, baking powder, sugar, butter and salt in a food processor until crumbly. Add beer and process in bursts to form a soft dough.

Preheat oven to 210°C. Turn dough out onto a well-floured surface and knead until smooth, adding extra flour if needed. Divide dough into four balls, place on greased oven trays and flatten slightly. Brush with a little water and slash tops with a knife. Bake for 10 minutes. Reduce oven to 180°C and bake for 10 minutes more, or until cooked. Cool on a wire rack.

Brown soda bread

1⅔ cups wholemeal self-raising flour, plus extra for sprinkling
1⅔ cups unbleached self-raising flour
1 teaspoon bicarbonate of soda
3 cups buttermilk

Preheat oven to 190°C. Sift flours and soda into a large bowl, add the husks to the bowl and make a well in the centre. Add 625 ml of the buttermilk and mix with a knife to form a soft dough, adding some of the remaining buttermilk if required.

Turn dough onto a floured surface and knead gently and briefly. Form dough into a 20 cm round and place on a greased baking tray. Score a deep cross with a floured knife one-third the depth of the dough. Lightly brush with water and sprinkle with a little more flour. Bake for 20–30 minutes, or until bread sounds hollow when tapped.

Soy and linseed loaf

½ cup pearl barley
7 g sachet dried yeast
1 teaspoon caster sugar
155 ml warm water
1 teaspoon salt
1 tablespoon linseeds
2 tablespoons soy flour
2 tablespoons gluten flour
1 cup wholemeal bread flour
2½ cups white bread flour
2 tablespoons olive oil
155 ml warm water, extra

Brush a 26 x 10 cm bread tin with oil. Put barley in a saucepan with 2 cups water, bring to the boil and boil for 20 minutes, or until softened. Drain.

Place the yeast, sugar and 155 ml warm water in a small bowl and mix well. Leave in a warm, draught-free place for 10 minutes, or until frothy.

Place barley, salt, linseeds, soy and gluten flours, wholemeal flour and 2 cups of the white flour in a large bowl. Make a well and add yeast mixture, oil and extra 155 ml warm water. Mix with a wooden spoon to a soft dough. Turn out onto a floured surface and knead for 10 minutes, or until smooth and elastic. Incorporate enough of the remaining flour until the dough is no longer sticky. Place dough in an oiled bowl and brush dough with oil. Cover with plastic wrap or a damp tea towel and leave in a warm, draught-free place for 45 minutes, or until doubled in size. Knock down dough by punching it lightly and knead for 2–3 minutes.

Pat dough into a 24 x 20 cm rectangle. Roll up firmly from the long side and place, seam-side down, in bread tin. Cover with plastic wrap or a damp tea towel and set aside in a warm, draught-free place for 1 hour, or until risen to the top of the tin. Meanwhile, preheat oven to 200°C.

Brush dough with water and make two slits on top. Bake for 30 minutes or until golden. Remove from the tin and cool on a wire rack.

State President's visit to Northern Tablelands, c1930

Jams
and
confectionery

Cumquat marmalade

1 kg cumquats
3 tablespoons lemon juice
1.25 kg sugar

Cut cumquats in half lengthways, reserving any pips, slice thinly and put in a large glass or ceramic bowl with 1.25 litres water. Tie pips securely in a square of muslin and add to bowl. Cover and refrigerate overnight.

Put cumquats, water, muslin bag and lemon juice in a large saucepan and bring to the boil. Reduce heat and simmer, covered, for 30–45 minutes or until fruit is tender. Add sugar and stir over low heat, without boiling, for 5 minutes or until dissolved. Return to a rapid boil, stirring often, for 20 minutes or until mixture jells. Discard muslin bag. Pour into hot, sterilised jars, seal and label.

Seville orange marmalade

4 Seville oranges (about 1.25 kg)
2–2.25 kg sugar

Scrub oranges under warm water, then cut in quarters. Slice thinly, retaining pips. Tie pips in a small square of muslin. Place oranges and muslin bag in large non-metallic bowl, add 2 litres water and leave to soak overnight.

Transfer fruit, water and muslin bag to a large saucepan. Bring to boil, reduce heat and simmer, covered, for 45 minutes or until fruit is tender.

Measure fruit mixture and for every 1 cup, add 1 cup sugar. Stir over low heat until sugar is dissolved then boil rapidly for 30 minutes or until mixture jells, removing any scum during cooking. Discard muslin bag. Pour into hot, sterilised jars, seal and label.

Three-fruit marmalade

1 grapefruit, finely sliced
1 orange, finely sliced
1 lemon, finely sliced
Seeds from sliced fruit
2.2 kg white sugar

Use fresh, clean-skinned fruit, as blemishes will show through. Remove seeds and tie in a small muslin bag. Place in a large saucepan with sliced fruit and soak in 2.5 litres water overnight. The next day, boil mixture for about 20 minutes, until pulp is soft. Add sugar. Boil quickly for another 30–40 minutes until it jells. Beware, there is only 1 or 2 minutes between cooked and over-cooked jam. Pour into hot, sterilised jars, seal and label.

Foolproof marmalade

900 g any citrus fruit or combination of citrus fruits
1.8 kg sugar
1 litre boiling water

Slice fruit finely, placing seeds in a separate container, and pour boiling water over both. Leave overnight. Add seed water to fruit, add 2 litres cold water and simmer slowly until tender. Gradually add sugar, stirring until dissolved. Boil rapidly until the mixture jells. When cooked, leave for at least 10 minutes before bottling in warm, sterilised jars, otherwise the fruit will rise to the top.

NOTE: Only make up to 1½ times this quantity at any one time; any more takes too long to jell and thickens and darkens in colour. Use freshly picked fruit. Older fruit darkens and does not produce a good jell.

Lime and ginger marmalade

16 large limes
1.3 kg sugar
2 teaspoons finely grated fresh ginger

Slice limes thinly and discard seeds. Place in a bowl, cover with 1.5 litres water and stand overnight. Pour into pan and simmer for about 1 hour or until soft. Add sugar and stir over high heat until dissolved. Boil rapidly, uncovered and without stirring, for approximately 15 minutes, until a teaspoon of mixture jells on a cold saucer. Remove from heat, add ginger and stand for 10 minutes before pouring into hot sterilised jars and sealing.

Plum and star anise jam

1 kg plums, quartered
1 kg sugar
½ cup lemon juice
3 star anise
1 teaspoon ground ginger

Combine ingredients in a large saucepan. Bring to the boil, stirring until sugar has dissolved. Reduce heat and simmer for 35–40 minutes, stirring frequently, until the mixture jells. Remove any froth from the surface of the jam and remove whole star anise with a metal spoon. Pour jam into hot, sterilised jars, seal and label.

Orange and peach jam

3 kg peaches, preferably yellow
Zest and juice of 3 oranges
2 kg sugar

Peel and slice peaches. Place peaches, 1 cup water and orange zest and juice in a pan. Cook for about 45 minutes. Remove from heat before adding sugar and stir to dissolve. Dissolve sugar before bringing jam to the boil. Boil briskly until jam jells. Pour into hot, sterilised jars, seal and label.

Mulberry and apple jam

2 kg mulberries, including some red ones
4 granny smith apples, grated
2 kg sugar

Place crushed or blended mulberries in a pan. Add the apple and bring to the boil, stirring constantly for 30 minutes. Heat sugar; add to fruit and boil for a further 20 minutes. Seeds should be soft. Cook until jam jells, then pour into hot, sterilised jars, seal and label.

Apricot jam

1 kg apricots (about 20)
1 kg sugar

Halve apricots and remove stones. Put apricots in a large saucepan with 375 ml water. Bring to the boil, stirring, for 20 minutes, or until the fruit has softened.

Add sugar to pan and stir, without boiling, for 5 minutes, or until all the sugar has dissolved. Return to the boil and cook for 20 minutes, stirring often. Remove any scum during cooking with a slotted spoon. When the jam falls from a wooden spoon in thick sheets without dripping, start testing for setting point by placing a spoonful on a cold saucer.

Once jam jells, pour into hot, sterilised jars, seal and label.

Store in a cool, dark place for 6–12 months. Once opened, the jam will keep in the fridge for 6 weeks.

Fig jam

1 kg figs
1 kg sugar
1 teaspoon ground ginger
Juice of 1 lemon

Remove stalks from figs. Cut figs roughly; do not peel. Use half the sugar to cover figs, stir well and allow to stand until juice rises. Place in a heavy-based pot over a moderately high heat and bring to the boil. Stir fruit off bottom of pot. Cook until tender. Add remaining sugar, ginger and lemon and cook for about 15 minutes or until jam jells on a cold saucer. When cooked, fruit has a tendency to sink and juice rises. Remove from heat. Pour into hot, sterilised jars, seal and label.

Strawberry jam

1.5 kg strawberries
1.25 kg sugar
½ cup lemon juice

Hull strawberries and put in a large saucepan with sugar, lemon juice and ½ cup water. Warm gently, without boiling, and stirring carefully with a wooden spoon. Try not to break the fruit up too much.

Increase heat, without boiling, and continue stirring for 10 minutes, until sugar has completely dissolved. Increase heat and boil without stirring for 20 minutes, or until mixture jells. Remove from heat and leave for 5 minutes, then remove any froth that has formed on the surface. Pour into hot, sterilised jars, label and seal.

NOTE: Above method can also be used with raspberries; you will need 1.5 kg sugar and ¼ cup lemon juice to each 1.5 kg fruit.

Quandong jam

500 g stoned quandongs
500 g sugar
Water
1 apple, peeled, cored and diced (optional)

Wash fruit and remove the stones. Weigh the fruit. Place in a large pot, cover with water and boil until pulpy. If necessary, add more water until all fruit is cooked thoroughly. The amount of water varies depending on how much the fruit absorbs. Then add sugar, and boil for approximately 20 minutes or until it jells into a thick jam consistency. An apple added before cooking will reduce the tartness of the flavour. Pour into hot, sterilised jars, seal and label.

Caramels

125 g butter or margarine
250 g brown sugar
400 g tin sweetened condensed milk
2 tablespoons golden syrup

Melt butter in a saucepan, then add sugar, condensed milk and golden syrup and heat until boiling. Stir constantly until mixture leaves sides of pan (10–20 minutes). Pour into a greased slab tin. Mark into squares when cooling. Cool in refrigerator. Break when cold and wrap.

Butterscotch

200 g brown sugar
100 g butter
Vanilla or almond essence

Lightly grease a 27 x 17 cm slice tray with butter. Place sugar in a saucepan with butter, essence and 125 ml water. Boil, stirring, for 10 minutes or until thick and creamy. Pour into the tray. When it starts to set, mark into small squares with a knife, then refrigerate. Break when cold.

Toffee

3 cups sugar
1 tablespoon vinegar

Place ingredients in a saucepan, add 1 cup of water and heat until sugar dissolves, then boil for 15 minutes. Remove from heat. When bubbles disappear, pour carefully into patty cases. Allow to set.

Apricot coconut balls

250 g dried apricots, finely chopped
2 tablespoons brandy or rum
½ cup cream
250 g white chocolate, chopped
¼ cup ground almonds
1 cup sweet biscuit crumbs
¾ cup desiccated coconut

Combine apricots and brandy in a bowl, cover, and stand for at least 10 minutes. Place cream in a small pan and bring to the boil. Remove from the heat. Add white chocolate and stir until melted. Add undrained apricots, almonds and biscuit crumbs and mix well. Refrigerate until mixture is firm enough to handle. Roll teaspoonfuls of mixture into small balls and toss in coconut. Refrigerate until ready to serve. Can be stored in refrigerator for up to 2 weeks.

Rum balls

400 g sweetened condensed milk
250 g crushed milk coffee biscuits
1 cup desiccated coconut, plus extra for sprinkling
3 tablespoons cocoa
3 dessertspoons rum, alcoholic substitute or vanilla

Mix all ingredients except extra coconut. Roll into small balls, then roll in extra coconut. Chill in refrigerator and store in an airtight container.

Creamy coconut ice

500 g icing sugar, sifted
250 g desiccated coconut
2 egg whites, slightly beaten
125 g Copha, melted
1 teaspoon vanilla
Pink food colouring

Mix dry ingredients with egg whites, Copha and vanilla. Press half the mixture in a greased slice tin, then add pink colouring to the other half and press on top of non-coloured mixture. Refrigerate.

Peanut brittle

125 g shelled peanuts or flaked toasted almonds
3 cups sugar
1 tablespoon vinegar

Grease a 20 x 30 cm slice tin. Spread nuts on tin. Place sugar, vinegar and 1 cup water in a saucepan, heat until sugar dissolves, then boil for 15 minutes. Remove from heat, wait for bubbles to disappear, then pour over peanuts. Leave to set. When cold, break into pieces.

Chocolate strawberries

250 g strawberries
125 g dark chocolate
15 g Copha

Wash strawberries well and allow to dry. Place chopped chocolate and Copha in top of double saucepan. Stir over simmering water until melted. Remove from heat and allow to cool. Using tongs or fingers to hold each strawberry, dip into the chocolate to coat the bottom half of the strawberry. Drain off excess chocolate. Place on a tray lined with aluminium foil. Allow to set.

Neverfail marshmallow

2 cups caster sugar
1 tablespoon gelatine
Colouring and flavouring, as desired
Desiccated coconut, to decorate

Mix sugar and gelatine in a large saucepan. Add 1½ cups water and stir well. Stand for 5 minutes, then bring to the boil. Boil rapidly for 5 minutes. Allow to cool. When mixture shows signs of setting, beat well until thick and white. While beating, add colouring and flavouring. Pour into a greased lamington tin and leave to set overnight. Cut into squares and roll in coconut.

This recipe can be used for snowballs or as a topping for biscuits or slices.

Rocky road

250 g pink and white marshmallows, halved
160 g unsalted peanuts, roughly chopped
105 g glacé cherries, halved
1 cup shredded coconut
350 g dark chocolate, chopped

Line the base and two opposite sides of a shallow 20 cm square cake tin with foil.

Put marshmallows, peanuts, cherries and coconut into a large bowl and mix until well combined.

Melt chocolate in a heatproof bowl over a saucepan of simmering water. Stir occasionally until the chocolate is melted.

Add the chocolate to the marshmallow mixture and toss until well combined. Spoon into the cake tin and press evenly over the base. Refrigerate for several hours, or until set. Carefully lift out of the tin, then peel away the foil and cut the rocky road into small pieces. Store in an airtight container in the refrigerator.

Hard caramels

220 g sugar
90 g unsalted butter
2 tablespoons golden syrup or dark corn syrup
⅓ cup liquid glucose
90 ml condensed milk
250 g dark chocolate, chopped

Grease the base and sides of a 20 cm square cake tin, then line with baking paper and grease the paper. Combine sugar, butter, syrup, glucose and milk in a heavy-based saucepan. Stir over medium heat without boiling until the butter has melted and the sugar has dissolved completely. Brush sugar crystals from the sides of the pan with a wet pastry brush. Bring to the boil, reduce heat slightly and boil, stirring, for about 10–15 minutes, or until a teaspoon of mixture dropped into cold water reaches hard ball stage (forming a firm ball that holds its shape). If using a sugar thermometer, the mixture must reach 122°C. Remove from heat immediately. Pour into tin and leave to cool. While caramel is still warm, mark into 2.5-cm squares with an oiled knife. When cold, cut through completely into squares.

Line two baking trays with foil. Melt chocolate in a small heatproof bowl over a saucepan of simmering water. Stir until the chocolate has melted. Remove from the heat and cool slightly. Using two forks, dip the caramels one at a time into the chocolate to coat. Lift out, drain the excess chocolate, then place on the trays and leave to set.

Chocolate clusters

125 g dark chocolate melts
125 g white chocolate melts
⅔ cup mixed dried fruit
125 g glacé ginger, chopped
30 g dark chocolate melts, extra, melted
30 g white chocolate melts, extra, melted

Put the dark chocolate in a heatproof bowl. Bring a saucepan of water to the boil, then remove from heat. Sit the bowl over the pan, making sure the base does not touch the water. Stir occasionally until the chocolate has melted. Cool slightly. In another bowl, repeat with the white chocolate.

Stir the mixed fruit into the dark chocolate. Combine the ginger with the white chocolate. Drop spoonfuls of the mixtures onto foil-lined trays, and leave to set at room temperature. Drizzle with the extra melted chocolate.

Rich chocolate truffles

¾ cup thick cream
400 g dark chocolate, grated
70 g unsalted butter, chopped
2 tablespoons Cointreau or other orange-flavoured liqueur
Cocoa powder, for rolling

Place cream in a small saucepan and bring to the boil. Remove from heat, add chocolate and stir in until completely melted. Add butter and stir until melted and combined. Stir in Cointreau. Transfer to a large bowl, cover and refrigerate for several hours or overnight, or until firm enough to roll.

Quickly roll tablespoons of the mixture into balls, and chill until firm. Roll the balls in the cocoa, shake off any excess and return to the refrigerator. Serve at room temperature.

NOTE: The truffle mixture can be made and rolled up to 2 weeks ahead. You will need to roll the balls in cocoa again close to serving time.

Chocolate mallow fudge

70 g butter, chopped
150 g dark chocolate, chopped
250 g white marshmallows
1 teaspoon vanilla
50 g milk chocolate

Line base and two long sides of an 8 x 26 cm loaf tin with foil. Put butter, dark chocolate and marshmallows in a saucepan and stir constantly over low heat until chocolate and marshmallows have melted. Remove pan from heat and stir in the vanilla.

Pour mixture into the tin and refrigerate for several hours or overnight, until firm.

Remove fudge from tin and remove the foil. Cut into 2 cm slices, then cut each slice into three pieces. Melt the milk chocolate and drizzle over the fudge, then set aside until set. Makes about 40.

Manly Branch, c1950s

Sauces
and
preserves

Mint sauce

750 ml brown vinegar
600 g sugar
1 dessertspoon salt, or to taste
2 bunches chopped mint

Combine all ingredients and boil for 15–20 minutes. Cool before bottling. Will keep for a few months if stored in a refrigerator. When ready to use, simply add a little water when warming.

Cheese sauce

3 tablespoons cornflour
1 level teaspoon mustard
1 litre low-fat milk
1 bay leaf
Pepper
1 cup grated tasty cheese

Mix cornflour and mustard to a smooth paste, using a little of the milk. Place remainder of milk and the bay leaf in a medium-sized saucepan and heat gently until mixture boils. Remove from heat and allow mixture to stand for a few minutes. Remove bay leaf. Stir in cornflour mixture and return saucepan to the heat, stirring constantly, until the sauce reaches boiling point. Reduce heat to simmer and continue to cook for 2 minutes, stirring all the time. Remove from heat and season to taste with pepper. Stir in cheese and use as required.

Cream sauce (with variations)

1 tablespoon butter
1 tablespoon flour
Salt, to taste
⅛ teaspoon pepper
1 cup milk

Melt butter over low heat in a saucepan. Blend in flour and salt and pepper, then cook over a low heat, stirring, until the mixture is smooth and bubbling. Remove from heat and stir in the milk. Bring to the boil, stirring constantly. Boil for 1 minute. This makes a thin cream sauce. To thicken, double the amount of butter and flour.

VARIATIONS:

Cheese sauce: Make sauce of medium consistency. Add ½ cup grated mature cheese, stirring until cheese melts.

Caper sauce: Make sauce of medium consistency. After sauce thickens, add 1–2 tablespoons finely chopped capers, 1 tablespoon vinegar, pinch of sugar, and salt and pepper to taste.

Egg sauce: Make sauce of medium consistency. Add 2 chopped hard-boiled eggs, pinch of nutmeg, and salt and pepper to taste. Reheat gently.

Mushroom sauce: Make sauce of medium consistency. Add 60–90 g sliced mushrooms sautéed in butter.

Onion sauce: Make sauce of medium consistency. Add 2 chopped and lightly cooked onions. Sprinkle with nutmeg.

Mustard sauce: Make sauce of medium consistency. Add 1–2 teaspoons mustard and 1 dessertspoon of wine or cider vinegar, salt and pepper. Reheat gently.

Parsley sauce: Make sauce of medium consistency. Add 3–5 tablespoons chopped parsley.

Barbecue sauce

1 small onion, finely chopped
Oil, for frying
1 tablespoon malt vinegar
1 tablespoon Worcestershire sauce
1 tablespoon brown sugar
½ cup tomato sauce

Fry the onion in a little oil over low heat for 3 minutes, or until soft but not browned. Add vinegar, Worcestershire sauce, sugar and tomato sauce. Bring to the boil and then reduce the heat and simmer for about 3 minutes, or until sauce has slightly thickened. Serve barbecue sauce warm or at room temperature with meatballs or sausages.

Chilli dipping sauce

1 tablespoon peanut oil
1 garlic clove, crushed
¼ cup sweet chilli sauce
2 tablespoons soy sauce
2 tablespoons sherry
1 tablespoon lemon juice

Heat the oil in a small saucepan over medium heat. Cook the garlic until just golden. Add the chilli sauce, soy sauce, sherry and lemon juice and stir until smooth and heated through. Serve warm with Thai starters such as spring rolls and fish cakes.

Dill sauce

½ cup plain yoghurt
½ cup sour cream
1 tablespoon horseradish cream
2 tablespoons chopped dill
3 spring onions (scallions), finely chopped
Salt and pepper

Combine yoghurt, sour cream and horseradish in a bowl and stir until creamy. Add dill and spring onion and mix well. Season with salt and pepper. Serve chilled, with fish, or spoon over steamed new potatoes.

Tartare sauce

1½ cups whole-egg mayonnaise
1 tablespoon finely chopped onion
1 teaspoon lemon juice
1 tablespoon chopped gherkins
1 teaspoon chopped capers
¼ teaspoon dijon mustard
1 tablespoon finely chopped parsley

Put mayonnaise, onion, lemon juice, gherkins, capers, mustard and parsley in a bowl. Mix well and season with salt and pepper. Serve with deep-fried battered or crumbed fish or calamari rings.

Caramel sauce

1 cup sugar

Bring 1 cup water to boil in a medium pan. Add sugar and stir until dissolved. Return pan to heat and bring to the boil. Cook rapidly (without stirring) until golden brown, occasionally brushing sugar crystals from inside of pan with a pastry brush dipped in cold water. Place pan in sink and with hand covered in towel, add ½ cup water to the pan. (Mixture will splatter.) Return pan to heat and stir until caramel has dissolved. Chill sauce before serving.

Strawberry sauce

250 g strawberries
2 tablespoons caster sugar
1 tablespoon lemon or orange juice

Hull strawberries and place in a blender with sugar and juice. Blend until smooth; strain if desired. Chill before serving.

Hot chocolate fudge sauce

1 cup cream
30 g butter
1 tablespoon golden syrup
200 g chopped dark chocolate

In a small saucepan, combine all ingredients and stir over low heat until butter and chocolate have melted and the mixture is smooth. Serve sauce hot or at room temperature. Makes 2 cups.

Berry sauce

300 g mixed raspberries and blackberries
250 g strawberries, hulled and halved
1 tablespoon sugar
½ teaspoon grated lemon zest
Vanilla ice-cream, to serve

Put all berries in a saucepan. Gently stir over low heat until heated through. Add the sugar and lemon zest and stir until the sugar has dissolved and the liquid is syrupy. Serve warm, with vanilla ice-cream.

Passionfruit sauce

¾ cup passionfruit pulp (6–8 passionfruit)
¼ cup orange juice
2 tablespoons caster sugar
1 tablespoon cornflour

Strain the passionfruit to separate the juice and seeds — you will need 125 ml of juice and 1½ tablespoons of seeds. Put passionfruit juice, seeds, orange juice and sugar in a small saucepan.

Mix the cornflour with ¼ cup water until smooth, then add to the passionfruit mixture. Stir over medium heat until the mixture boils and thickens. Serve warm or cold, with steamed puddings, pancakes or waffles.

Lemon curd

2 eggs
2 cups sugar
Zest and juice of 2 lemons
60 g butter

Place all ingredients in a double boiler and cook over water until thick, stirring occasionally. Strain, bottle and seal while hot.

Peach relish

6 cups chopped ripe freestone peaches
6 cups chopped brown onions
750 ml brown vinegar
3 dessertspoons salt
3 dessertspoons curry powder
6 cups sugar
Cornflour (about 2 tablespoons depending on how much
  juice the peaches give)

Plunge peaches into cold water to remove skins easily. Stone and chop fruit into medium cubes. Measure 6 cups and place in pot with chopped onions and most of the vinegar (saving some to mix with the cornflour later to thicken the mixture).

Stir over medium heat to prevent burning, and cook till softened. Add salt, then curry powder, then sugar. Cook till tender. Thicken with cornflour blended with the reserved vinegar. Bring to boil, stir and cook 10 minutes. Bottle while hot into warm sterilised bottles and seal using plastic lids.

Mixed mustard pickles

1 kg cucumber (apple cucumber or burpless Lebanese)
1½ kg zucchini
500 g carrots
250 g pumpkin
500 g brown onions
200 g green tomatoes (optional)
1½ tablespoons cooking salt
1.5 litres white vinegar
25 g turmeric
1½ teaspoons curry powder
1½ teaspoons mustard powder
1 teaspoon white pepper
Approximately 3 cups white sugar (depending on your taste)

Grate the vegetables (this can be quickly done using a food processor) and place in a large saucepan. Sprinkle with salt, add vinegar and refrigerate for at least 2 hours or overnight.

Bring to boil, stirring occasionally so as not to burn on the bottom of the pan. Reduce heat and gently simmer for 30 minutes, then add turmeric, curry powder, mustard powder, white pepper and the sugar. Boil for another 30 minutes.

Pour into jars that have been warmed a little and place lids on jars while hot so that they seal.

NOTE: The preparation and cooking can take up to 3 hours but the recipe will yield 6 kg (11 cups) of mixture, which will fill about 15 medium-sized jars.

Some of the above vegetables
can be replaced with others such as
green tomatoes or even cauliflower.

Peach and apple relish

2 kg firm peaches
1 kg granny smith apples
500 g onions
750 g brown sugar
1 teaspoon cloves
1 teaspoon peppercorns
1 teaspoon allspice
900 ml vinegar
500 g raisins or sultanas
2 tablespoons salt
1 level teaspoon ground ginger
1 clove garlic, crushed

In a large saucepan, place finely chopped peaches, apples and onions. Add sugar and stand overnight. Tie the cloves, peppercorns and allspice in a muslin bag. Add the vinegar, raisins or sultanas, salt, ginger, garlic and spice bag and cook slowly over a medium heat until relish is very thick. This will take 2½–3 hours. Remove spice bag. Bottle while hot and seal. Makes 4 cups.

Grapefruit butter

1 tablespoon grated grapefruit zest
1 cup grapefruit juice
1¼ cups caster sugar
125 g butter, roughly chopped
3 eggs
2 teaspoons gelatine

Place zest, juice, caster sugar, ½ cup water and roughly chopped butter in the top of a double saucepan. Stir over direct heat until mixture comes to the boil, reduce heat and simmer uncovered for 3 minutes. Remove pan from heat and allow to cool slightly. Place eggs in a bowl, beat until frothy, then gradually add to grapefruit mixture. Place pan over a saucepan of simmering water and stir for 20 minutes or until mixture is thick. Dissolve gelatine in 2 tablespoons water and add to mixture. Pour into hot sterilised jars and seal. Store in a refrigerator.

Quince paste

3 large quinces
800 g sugar, approximately

Wash quinces, then place in a saucepan and add enough water to cover. Bring to the boil, then reduce the heat and simmer for 30 minutes, or until tender. Drain and leave until they are cool enough to handle. Peel and core the quinces, then push them through a sieve, food mill or potato ricer, discarding the solids. Weigh quince pulp and place in a heavy-based saucepan. Measure the same weight of sugar and add to the saucepan. Simmer over low heat, stirring occasionally, for 3½–4½ hours, or until very thick, taking care not to let the mixture burn. Remove from the heat and allow to cool a little.

Line a 28 x 18 cm rectangular cake tin or dish with plastic wrap, then pour the quince mixture into the tin and set aside to cool. The quince paste can be kept for several months in a tightly sealed container in the fridge. Serve with cheese and bread or crackers, or with game such as pheasant.

Tomato chutney

1 kg ripe tomatoes, peeled and coarsely chopped
3 onions, coarsely chopped
2 green apples, peeled and coarsely chopped
3 peaches, peeled, halved, stoned and coarsely chopped
2¾ cups dark brown sugar
2 cups white vinegar
1 tablespoon salt
1 teaspoon mixed spice
1 teaspoon Mexican chilli powder

Place all ingredients in a large pan or boiler. Bring slowly to boil and simmer for about 2 hours, uncovered, until mixture is thick. Stir occasionally. Remove from heat and stand for 5 minutes. Pour into hot sterilised jars and seal immediately.

Exhibition tips

Biscuits

Keep within the class named. Do not use too much shortening as biscuits become greasy; use about half as much fat as flour. A mixture of self-raising flour with plain flour or cornflour gives the best results. Roll thinly and cut into dainty shapes or use a biscuit forcer, as this attracts more credit than drop biscuits. Bake slowly to prevent breakage and loss of shape. To present correctly, arrange a few biscuits of each variety, whether plain or fancy, on a plate, unless a box of biscuits is stated. Biscuits can be stored for a week in an airtight container.

Butter cakes

Use butter or first-grade table margarine. All ingredients should be at room temperature, or slightly warm butter, milk and eggs in hot water. For the quick-mix method, butter should be very soft, but not melted. If an electric mixer is used, beat in flour on speed 2 for up to 2 minutes. When mixing, add flour and milk alternately, beginning and ending with flour. Vigorously beat flour that contains gluten; this will result in a fine texture. Before placing in an oven, make a graduated hollow in the centre of large cakes, to assist even rising. Use a moderate oven, as a hot oven seizes the sides, causing the cake to set too soon, dome and crack. A cake with a small crack, that is otherwise good, is better than a smooth-topped one which is sodden inside. Cool cake in pan for up to 15 minutes before turning out. A rainbow cake is a butter cake and must be layered from the base in the order of chocolate, pink and white. Butter cakes cut better when 1 day old.

Chocolate cakes

This should be a block cake, light but not crumbly, and even in texture and in colour (dark reddish-brown) on the base and sides. It should not have large holes or wet streaks. Flavouring must be chocolate with no trace of excess soda. Cracks are disregarded, if cake is otherwise good. Use any shape pan. A layer cake with cream is not a chocolate cake. Chocolate cake may be iced with chocolate icing and decorated simply.

Dark fruit cakes

Some competitions specify a 20 cm size pan. If no size is given, a very large cake does not gain more points than a smaller one. Cake should be smooth on top, well risen, but not domed. A slight crack is not a defect. Should be firm with more fruit than cake, but not dry. Fruit should be evenly distributed. Cake is best if cut up before serving. It should not have damp patches, sodden streaks or holes. The flavour should be a rich fruit, without too much spice.

The cake needs about 3 weeks to mature; a light fruit cake can be made 2–3 days early. Stand the cake in the tin until cold, to avoid breaking.

Lamingtons

Judges should state their preferred size; most prefer lamingtons not higher than 3.7 cm, but some allow 4.5 cm. Should be a butter cake mixture. Texture should be fine and moist. Leave cake until the next day before cutting. Icing should be even and well flavoured, and the coconut should be fresh, not soaked or covered in chocolate. When cut, coating should not have soaked into the cake.

Scones

Present no more than 6 unbuttered scones. Shortening should be one-tenth the weight of flour; too much makes scones crisp. Avoid too much liquid and too much handling. Glaze tops with milk, or milk and egg. Very large scones are not as attractive as smaller ones, and round scones are preferred to other shapes. Use a 2.5 cm deep tin and stand scones close together, to retain steam and soften scones. Remove from oven and wrap in a clean towel. Remove excess flour or grease from scone base. Bake and cool just before exhibition. Break scones open, never cut them.

Sponges

Use fresh eggs. A temperature of 21°C gives best results. The cake should be made just long enough to cool before exhibition. Layers should be even in height (weigh empty pans, then weigh again when filled with mixture) with no overhanging edges or tucks. The top should be smooth, not sticky, and without sugar or soda spots, or crack marks. Some judges allow a fine sprinkling of icing sugar, but most prefer a plain top. Grease and flour tin, then shake off excess flour. Mix beaten eggs and castor sugar until sugar dissolves, as the texture of the sponge is thus determined. Sift flour at least three times, to incorporate as much air as possible. Make sure liquid is well blended in the mixture, or the top of the cake will be streaky. Do not place the scraping from the bowl in the centre of the layer, as this could show when cut. Divide mixture between two tins. When cooked, allow cake to stand in tin for a few minutes before turning out. Turn out onto a clean folded tea-towel, then turn right side up. If top remains on the tea-towel, the cake has a moist surface. If turned onto a wire rack, the wire would mark the top of the cake.

Sultana cakes

The crust should be a lighter brown than that of a fruit cake. Colour and fruit distribution should be even. There should be more cake than fruit. Do not use spices. If lemon essence is used, it should not be too strong.

Catering hints

Although some caterers have different ideas on quantities, these quantities are tried, tested and treasured. We hope this information prevents over-catering, or even worse, preparing too little.

TEA 30 g for 6; 250 g for 50 (30 g equals about 7 teaspoons). For tea or coffee, use 2 litres for 40 people.

INSTANT COFFEE 125 g makes 50 small cups; 500 g coffee makes 250 white or 130–150 black coffees.

SUGAR 500 g sugar serves 50; 500 g loaf sugar equals approximately 112 blocks.

BUTTER 250 g butter per 1 kg loaf of bread; or combine 175 g creamed butter and 60 ml warm milk per 1 kg loaf of bread, which is more economical and easier to spread.

BREAD 680 g loaf makes 10 sandwiches or 25 slices to one loaf; 750 g loaf equals 12 double slices; 1 kg loaf equals 16 double slices; and 16 double slices cut in quarters serve 20 people. **Egg filling for sandwiches:** 6–8 hard-boiled eggs, mashed with butter and salt and pepper, per 1 kg loaf.

SOUP 8 litres serves 50 people, based on ¾–1 cup per person.

CHEESE 1 kg serves 50.

SALAD 6 large lettuces, shredded, serve 50; 1.25 kg tomatoes, thinly sliced, serve 50.

MEAT AND POULTRY 60–90 g cooked boned meat or poultry per person; 325 g per person for uncooked meat cuts off the bone. **Boneless cuts or sausages** up to 250 g each; **Chicken** 1.5 kg serves 6–8; one size 18 chicken serves 4 people; 9 kg chicken thighs equals about 70 pieces. **Ham** 7 medium tomatoes to 1 kg. **Sandwich meat** 50–300 g chopped or minced meat or chicken per 1 kg loaf. **Turkey** 9 kg serves 25 people.

CASSEROLE Serves 6–8.

RICE 500 g uncooked rice serves 16 when cooked; 1 cup uncooked rice yields 3 cups cooked rice.

VEGETABLES Beetroot 25 slices per 825 g can or 100 slices per 3 kg can. **Carrots** 1 kg, cut into rings, serves 20. **Peas** 2 kg frozen peas serves 30–35. **Potatoes** 3.25 kg cooked potato with extras serves 50; 3 kg potato (mashed) equals 30 good servings.

CAKES AND DESSERTS Cheesecake or tart 23 cm tart cuts into 10–12 pieces (1 serve per person). **Custard** 4.5 litres serves 50. **Fruit salad** One 900 g can serves 10–12 (½ cup each). **Ice-cream** 1 litre serves 8–10; 4 litres yields 35 scoops. **Pavlova** (based on 4 eggs) serves 10–12. **Small cakes and slices** provide 2 per person or 3 each for two people. **Sponges** (deep 20cm round sponges) Cut a small circle in the centre and cut into 10 slices.

Measuring up

OVEN TEMPERATURES

	Celsius	Fahrenheit	Gas mark
Very slow	120	250	1
Slow	150	300	2
Moderately slow	160	325	3
Moderate	180–190	350–375	4
Moderately hot	200–210	400–425	5
Hot	220–230	450–475	6
Very hot	240–250	500–525	7

DRY MEASURES   LIQUID MEASURES

Metric	Imperial	Metric	Imperial
30 g	1 oz	30 ml	1 fluid oz
60 g	2 oz	60 ml	2 fluid oz
90 g	3 oz	100 ml	3 fluid oz
155 g	5 oz	150 ml	5 fluid oz (¼ pint)
250 g	8 oz (1/2 lb)	250 ml	8 fluid oz
500 g	16 oz (1 lb)	500 ml	16 fluid oz
1 kg	32 oz (2 lb)	1000 ml (1 litre)	1¾ pints

Index

A
angel food cake 134
Anzac biscuits 174
apples
    apple and cinnamon cake 161
    apple dessert cake
      (microwave) 162
    apple pie 112
    apple slice 176
    baked apple pudding 112
    mulberry and apple
      jam 217
    peach and apple relish 239
    spiced apple cake 155
apricot coconut balls 221
apricot ginger fingers 177
apricot jam 218
apricot layer parfait 116
asparagus
    asparagus stir-fried with
      mustard 106
    chicken and asparagus stir-fry 86
    Swiss quiche 45
    veal with asparagus 66
avocado
    bacon and avocado salad 96
    guacamole 22

B
bacon
    bacon and avocado salad 96
    cheese and bacon straws 21
    chusuolettes 15
    egg and bacon quiche 50
    impossible pie 50

    pasta with bacon, tomato and
      olives 63
    potato bacon salad 92
    vegetable and bacon quiche 48
    zucchini slice 47
banana blueberry cake 135
banana cake 135
banana health bread 209
banana sponge 136
barbecue honey chicken wings 20
barbecue meatloaf 70
barbecue sauce 70, 232
beans
    cannellini bean salad 97
    green beans with tomato and
      olive oil 109
    oriental beef and beans 62
beef
    barbecue meatloaf 70
    beef and vegetable casserole 56
    Cornish pastie 71
    creamy beef stroganoff
      (microwave) 58
    goulash soup 28
    Hungarian goulash soup 29
    macaroni and mince slice 74
    meat patties (microwave) 60
    meatloaf (microwave) 60
    Mexican-style beef spareribs 80
    oriental beef and beans 62
    piquant country beef with herb
      scones 76
    sausage rolls 19
    savoury beef pie 67
    savoury potato empanadas 23

beer bread rolls 210
beetroot cake 137
berry sauce 235
biscuits
    Anzac biscuits 174
    apricot ginger fingers 177
    burnt butter 168
    cheese biscuits 168
    chocolate caramel shortbread 183
    custard cream 172
    ginger creams 169
    Irene's brown crunchies 170
    jam drops 169
    orange biscuits 170
    orange walnut shortbread 175
    passionfruit shortbread 190
    shortbread 171
Boxing Day salad 92
bread and butter pudding 113
breads
    banana health bread 209
    beer bread rolls 210
    brown soda bread 210
    damper 202
    soy and linseed loaf 211
    white loaf 207
    wholemeal bread 208
brown soda bread 210
brown sugar tart 117
brownies, cashew 198
bruschetta 17
    smoked salmon and caper 41
burnt butter biscuits 168
butter, grapefruit 240
butter cake, basic 136
butter milk pannacotta 116
butterscotch 220
butterscotch self-saucing pudding 119

C
cabbage, braised 99
cakes
    angel food cake 134
    apple and cinnamon cake 161
    apple dessert cake (microwave)
       162
    banana blueberry 135
    banana cake 135
    banana sponge 136
    basic butter cake 136
    beetroot cake 137
    carrot and sultana 138
    chocolate cake 134
    chocolate macaroon cake 140
    chocolate ripple cake 141
    crunchy coffee cake 139
    date loaf 132
    Dutch cake 142
    fruit cake 143
    fruit loaf 133
    ginger sponge 144
    honey roll 145
    Irene's date and walnut loaf 133
    Kentish cake 146
    lemon tea cake 147
    macaroon cake 148
    marble cake 149
    moist coconut cake 150
    Norwegian sour cream cake 146
    orange and almond cake 151
    peach blossom cake 159
    pineapple coconut cake 156
    pineapple upside-down cake 151
    potato chocolate cake 152
    potato fruit bun 165
    pumpkin fruit cake 153
    pumpkin loaf 132

quick light fruit cake 153
quick mix cake 162
rich mocha cake 154
shearers' cakes 171
spiced apple cake 155
sponge sandwich 156
sultana cake 163
two-at-a-time 165
wholemeal boiled fruit cake 164
wholemeal date and honey
   cake 157
cannellini bean salad 97
caper sauce 231
capsicum and tomato stew 104
caramel
   caramel sauce 234
   caramel slice 179
   caramels 220
   hard caramels 225
carrots
   carrot and sultana cake 138
   ginger carrot soup 27
   honey-glazed carrots 103
cashew brownies 198
cheese
   bruschetta 17
   cheese and bacon straws 21
   cheese biscuits 168
   cheese sauce 74, 230
   cheese scones 206
   eggplant parmigiana 82
   honeycomb cheesecake slice 194
   mascarpone and lime torte 114
   pastizzi 69
   potato moussaka 65
   savoury cakes 13
   savoury sticks 13
   turkey and brie triangles 39

cherry strudel 128
cherry and walnut slice 180
chicken
   barbecue honey chicken wings 20
   chicken and asparagus stir-fry 86
   chicken cacciatore 75
   chicken casserole with olives and
      tomato 83
   chicken in peanut sauce 57
   chicken pie 52
   chicken, rocket and walnut
      sandwiches 40
   chicken stock 26
   Greek-style roast chicken 73
   marinated chicken wings 10
   oven-fried mustard chicken 56
   spring chicken soup 26
   stuffed chicken breasts 68
chickpea and nut loaf 72
chilli dipping sauce 232
chilli nuts 18
chocolate
   chocolate cake 134
   chocolate caramel shortbread 183
   chocolate clusters 226
   chocolate fudge squares 173
   chocolate macaroon cake 140
   chocolate mallow fudge 227
   chocolate marshmallow slice 197
   chocolate peppermint slice 181
   chocolate ripple cake 141
   chocolate rough slice 182
   chocolate strawberries 223
   hot chocolate fudge sauce 235
   no-bake chocolate slice 188
   rich chocolate truffles 226
   self-saucing chocolate
      pudding 126

chusuolettes 15
chutney, tomato 241
coconut
    apricot coconut balls 221
    coconut delight 178
    creamy coconut ice 222
    lemon spiced coconut mini
      cupcakes 160
    moist coconut cake 150
    pineapple coconut cake 156
coffee cake, crunchy 139
coffee slice 184
coriander yoghurt 34
corn
    corn chowder 37
    corn fritters 16
    tuna, corn and onion quiche 49
Cornish pastie 71
cream, mock 145
cream sauces 231
crunchy coffee cake 139
crunchy tuna rolls 39
csipetke 29
cumquat marmalade 214
cupcakes, lemon spiced coconut 160
curry
  curried potato 102
  curried vegetable pasta salad 93
  curry rice puffs 10
  prawn curry 89
custard cream biscuits 172

D
damper 202
dates
    date and ginger slice 192
    date loaf 132
    Irene's date and walnut loaf 133

Nita's date slice 193
wholemeal date and honey
    cake 157
desserts
    apple pie 112
    apricot layer parfait 116
    baked apple pudding 112
    baked rice custard 120
    bread and butter pudding 113
    brown sugar tart 117
    butter milk pannacotta 116
    butterscotch self-saucing
      pudding 119
    cherry strudel 128
    Grandmother's pavlova 125
    ice cream cake 118
    khoshaf (dried fruit salad) 113
    lemon delicious 123
    mango fool 128
    mango and passionfruit
      pies 122
    mascarpone and lime torte 114
    passionfruit mousse 121
    pavlova roll 115
    peach pie 124
    rhubarb and pear crumble 127
    self-saucing chocolate
      pudding 126
dill sauce 233
dipping sauce, chilli 232
Dutch cake 142

E
easy fruit slice 185
eggplant
    eggplant parmigiana 82
    Moroccan eggplant 103

eggs
  chusuolettes 15
  egg and bacon quiche 50
  egg sauce 231
  pastizzi 69

F
fig jam 218
fish
  fish and cumin kebabs 85
  Nora's fish dish (microwave) 61
  salmon pâté 12
  savoury pie 44
  seafood pâté 14
  smoked salmon and caper
    bruschetta 41
  see also seafood; tuna
foolproof marmalade 215
fruit cake 143
  pumpkin 153
  quick light 153
  wholemeal boiled 164
fruit loaf 133
fruit and walnut slice 178
fudge, chocolate mallow 227

G
garlic
  Moroccan eggplant 103
  zucchini with garlic butter 101
ginger carrot soup 27
ginger creams 169
ginger fantasy bar 186
ginger sponge 144
gluten-free muffins 158
goulash soup 28
Grandmother's pavlova 125
grapefruit butter 240

Greek-style roast chicken 73
green beans with tomato and olive
  oil 109
guacamole 22

H
ham
  pea and ham soup 30
  zucchini slice 47
Helen's quick spinach quiche 44
herb mustard rolls 16
herb scones 76
honey roll 145
honeycomb cheesecake slice 194
honey-glazed carrots 103
hot chocolate fudge sauce 235
hot water pastry 71
Hungarian goulash soup 29

I
ice cream cake 118
icing
  chocolate 173
  lemon 142
impossible pie 50
Irene's brown crunchies 170
Irene's date and walnut loaf 133

J
jam
  apricot 218
  fig 218
  mulberry and apple 217
  orange and peach 217
  plum and star anise 216
  quandong 219
  strawberry 219
jam drops 169

Japanese golden mushroom soy soup 30
jumbuck stew 59
jungle scones 203

K
kebabs, fish and cumin 85
Kentish cake 146
khoshaf (dried fruit salad) 113

L
lamb
    jumbuck stew 59
    Lancashire hotpot 78
    rosemary-infused lamb and lentil
       casserole 88
    slow-cooked shanks 87
Lancashire hotpot 78
lattice cream slice 185
leek and potato soup 38
lemon curd 236
lemon delicious 123
lemon fruit slice 187
lemon icing 142
lemon slice 195
lemon spiced coconut cupcakes 160
lemon tea cake 147
lentils
    pumpkin and lentil soup 31
    rosemary-infused lamb and lentil
       casserole 88
    tomato, lentil and coriander
       soup 34
lime and ginger marmalade 216
lime juice 22

M
macaroni and mince slice 74
macaroon cake 148

mango fool 128
mango and passionfruit pies 122
marble cake 149
marmalade
    cumquat 214
    foolproof 215
    lime and ginger 216
    Seville orange 214
    three-fruit 215
marshmallow, neverfail 223
marshmallow bars 196
mascarpone and lime torte 114
meat patties (microwave) 60
meat sauce 74
meatloaf, barbecue 70
meatloaf (microwave) 60
Melba toasts 12
Mexican-style beef spareribs 80
microwave dishes
    apple dessert cake 162
    beef and vegetable casserole 56
    chicken in peanut sauce 57
    creamy beef stroganoff 58
    honey-glazed carrots 103
    meat patties 60
    meatloaf 60
    Nora's fish dish 61
    oriental ginger and cashew
       rice 104
    potato casserole 99
mint sauce 230
mocha cake, rich 154
mock cream 145
Moroccan eggplant 103
muesli slice 199
muffins
    gluten-free 158
    pumpkin 137

mulberry and apple jam 217
mushrooms
    fast mushroom soup 36
    impossible pie 50
    Japanese golden mushroom soy
      soup 30
    mushroom sauce 231
    tofu and shiitake soup 35
    tuna and mushroom sauce 69
mustard
    asparagus stir-fried with
      mustard 106
    herb mustard rolls 16
    mixed mustard pickles 238
    mustard sauce 231
    oven-fried mustard chicken 56
    veal with wine and mustard
      sauce 81

N
nameko 30
neverfail marshmallow 223
Nita's date slice 193
no-bake chocolate slice 188
Nora's fish dish (microwave) 61
Norwegian sour cream cake 146
nuts
    chicken in peanut sauce 57
    chickpea and nut loaf 72
    chilli nuts 18
    orange walnut shortbread 175
    oriental ginger and cashew rice 104
peanut brittle 222

O
olives
    chicken casserole with olives and
      tomato 83
    olive and onion tart 51
    pasta with bacon, tomato and
      olives 63
onions
    olive and onion tart 51
    onion sauce 231
opera house slice 189
orange
    orange and almond cake 151
    orange biscuits 170
    orange and peach jam 217
    orange walnut shortbread 175
    pumpkin and orange soup 32
    Seville orange marmalade 214
    spinach and orange salad 102
oriental beef and beans 62
oriental ginger and cashew rice
  (microwave) 104

P
parsley sauce 231
passionfruit sauce 236
passionfruit shortbread 190
passionfruit slice 191
pasta
    curried vegetable pasta
      salad 93
    macaroni and mince slice 74
    pasta with bacon, tomato and
      olives 63
    pasta with tuna and mushroom
      sauce 69
    pasta and vegetables 79
    tricolour pasta salad 108
pastizzi 69
pastry
    hot water 71
    sweet coffee 117

pâté
    salmon 12
    seafood 14
pavlova, Grandmother's 125
pavlova roll 115
pea and ham soup 30
peach and apple relish 239
peach blossom cake 159
peach pie 124
peach relish 237
peanut brittle 222
pickles, mixed mustard 238
pies
    chicken 52
    mango and passionfruit 122
    peach 124
    savoury 44
    savoury beef 67
    spinach 53
pineapple coconut cake 156
pineapple upside-down cake 151
piquant country beef with herb
  scones 76
plain scones 203
plum and star anise jam 216
pork
    barbecue meatloaf 70
    pork chops pizzaiola 84
    pork in creamy prune
      sauce 64
    sausage rolls 19
    savoury pinwheels 18
potatoes
    curried potato 102
    grated potato cakes 100
    leek and potato soup 38
    potato bacon salad 92

potato casserole (microwave) 99
potato chocolate cake 152
potato fruit bun 165
potato moussaka 65
potato scones 204
potatoes romanoff 100
savoury potato empanadas 23
Spanish tortilla 11
prawns
    prawn curry 89
    seafood salad and sauce 94
prune bars 197
pumpkin
    baked pumpkin casserole 98
    jumbuck stew 59
    pumpkin fruit cake 153
    pumpkin and lentil soup 31
    pumpkin loaf 132
    pumpkin muffins 137
    pumpkin and orange
      soup 32
    pumpkin scones 205
    pumpkin soup 31
    tomato pumpkin 105

Q
quandong jam 219
quiches
    egg and bacon 50
    Helen's quick spinach 44
    spinach 46
    Swiss quiche 45
    tuna, corn and onion 49
    tuna and silverbeet 46
    vegetable and bacon 48
quick mix cake 162
quince paste 241

R
raisin bars, old-fashioned 188
relish, peach 237, 239
rhubarb and pear crumble 127
rhubarb slice 187
rice
    baked rice custard 120
    oriental ginger and cashew rice 104
rich chocolate truffles 226
rocky road 224
rosemary-infused lamb and lentil
    casserole 88
rum balls 221

S
salads
    bacon and avocado 96
    Boxing Day salad 92
    cannellini bean 97
    curried vegetable pasta 93
    khoshaf (dried fruit salad) 113
    potato bacon salad 92
    roast tomato salad 98
    seafood salad and sauce 94
    spinach and orange 102
    spinach salad with dreamy creamy
        dressing 95
    tricolour pasta salad 108
    zucchini salad 94
salmon
    salmon pâté 12
    salmon and caper bruschetta 41
sandwiches, chicken rocket walnut 40
sauces
    barbecue 70, 232
    berry 235
    caramel 234
    cheese sauce 74, 230

cream (with variations) 231
dill sauce 233
hot chocolate fudge 235
meat sauce 74
mint sauce 230
passionfruit 236
strawberry 234
tartare sauce 233
tuna and mushroom 69
sausage rolls 19
savoury beef pie 67
savoury cakes 13
savoury pie 44
savoury pinwheels 18
savoury potato empanadas 23
savoury sticks 13
scones
    cheese 206
    jungle 203
    plain 203
    potato 204
    pumpkin 205
seafood see also fish
    prawn curry 89
    seafood pâté 14
    seafood salad and sauce 94
self-saucing butterscotch pudding 119
self-saucing chocolate pudding 126
Seville orange marmalade 214
shearers' cakes 171
shortbread 171
    chocolate caramel 183
    orange walnut 175
    passionfruit 190
slices
    apple 176
    caramel 179
    cashew brownies 198

cherry and walnut 180
chocolate fudge squares 173
chocolate marshmallow 197
chocolate peppermint 181
chocolate rough slice 182
coconut delight 178
coffee slice 184
date and ginger 192
easy fruit slice 185
fruit and walnut 178
ginger fantasy bar 186
honeycomb cheesecake 194
lattice cream slice 185
lemon fruit 187
lemon slice 195
marshmallow bars 196
muesli slice 199
no-bake chocolate slice 188
old-fashioned raisin bars 188
opera house slice 189
passionfruit slice 191
prune bars 197
rhubarb slice 187
sultana scone slice 205
soup
    corn chowder 37
    fast mushroom 36
    ginger carrot 27
    goulash soup 28
    Japanese golden mushroom soy
        soup 30
    leek and potato 38
    pea and ham soup 30
    pumpkin and lentil soup 31
    pumpkin and orange soup 32
    pumpkin soup 31
    spring chicken soup 26
    tofu and shiitake mushroom 35

tomato, lentil and coriander 34
    zucchini soup 33
soy and linseed loaf 211
Spanish tortilla 11
spiced apple cake 155
spinach
    Helen's quick spinach quiche 44
    spinach and orange salad 102
    spinach pie 53
    spinach quiche 46
    spinach salad with dreamy creamy
        dressing 95
sponge sandwich 156
spring chicken soup 26
stir-fries
    asparagus, with mustard 106
    chicken and asparagus 86
strawberries
    chocolate strawberries 223
    strawberry jam 219
    strawberry sauce 234
sultana cake 163
sultana scone slice 205
sweet coffee pastry 117
Swiss quiche 45

T
tartare sauce 233
three-fruit marmalade 215
toffee 220
tofu and shiitake mushroom
    soup 35
tomatoes
    bruschetta 17
    chicken cacciatore 75
    chicken casserole with olives and
        tomato 83
    eggplant parmigiana 82

pasta with bacon, tomato and
    olives 63
pork chops pizzaiola 84
roast tomato salad 98
tomato, lentil and coriander
    soup 34
tomato and capsicum stew 104
tomato chutney 241
tomato pumpkin 105
tortilla, Spanish 11
tricolour pasta salad 108
tuna
    crunchy tuna rolls 39
    tuna, corn and onion quiche 49
    tuna and mushroom sauce 69
    tuna and silverbeet quiche 46
    tuna toasties 15
turkey
    Boxing Day salad 92
    turkey and brie triangles 39
two-at-a-time cake 165

V
veal with asparagus 66
veal chops with sage and lemon 77
veal with wine and mustard sauce 81
vegetable and bacon quiche 48
vegetables
    asparagus stir-fried with
        mustard 106
    baked pumpkin casserole 98
    braised cabbage 99
    curried potato 102
    curried vegetable pasta salad 93
    eggplant parmigiana 82
    grated potato cakes 100
    green beans with tomato and olive
        oil 109

    with honey and soy 107
    honey-glazed carrots
        (microwave) 103
    Moroccan eggplant 103
    pasta and vegetables 79
    potatoes romanoff 100
    tomato and capsicum stew 104
    tomato pumpkin 105
    vegetable slice 105
    zucchini bake 101
    zucchini with garlic butter 101
venison, roast haunch of 66

W
white loaf 207
wholemeal boiled fruit cake 164
wholemeal bread 208
wholemeal date and honey cake 157

Y
yoghurt, coriander 34

Z
zucchini bake 101
zucchini salad 94
zucchini slice 47
zucchini soup 33